eat
taste
nourish

eat
taste
nourish

Fabulous food for body and soul

Zoe Bingley-Pullin

NEW
HOLLAND

First published in Australia in 2009 by
New Holland Publishers (Australia) Pty Ltd
Sydney • Auckland • London • Cape Town

1/66 Gibbes Street Chatswood NSW 2067 Australia
218 Lake Road Northcote Auckland New Zealand
86 Edgware Road London W2 2EA United Kingdom
80 McKenzie Street Cape Town 8001 South Africa

A record of this book is held at the National Library of Australia

ISBN 9781741108026

Publisher: Fiona Schultz and Linda Williams
Publishing Manager: Lliane Clarke
Senior Project Editor: Joanna Tovia
Designer: Tania Gomes
Photographs: Graeme Gillies
Food stylist: Georgina Dolling
Production Manager: Olga Dementiev
Printer: KHL Printing Co. Pte Ltd

10 9 8 7 6 5 4 3 2 1

With thanks to Country Road Homewares, Orson & Blake Woolhara and Porter's Paints for providing
fine tableware, paints and wallpapers.

Contents

Discovering the Joy of Good Food

When I was eighteen, fresh out of high school, I knew that my life would be devoted to good food. Creating delicious meals had been my passion and obsession for as long as I could remember. In fact, I was so certain food, nutrition and culinary arts would be at the centre of my life that I opted not to go straight to university after high school. Instead, I enrolled at the Le Cordon Bleu school in London to commence my training as a chef.

I learnt Parisian cooking at the school. I loved every moment of my studies and 'ate up' everything they taught me. Literally. The one aspect of my studies I did not love was gaining about 10 kilograms (22 pounds).

The cuisine we learnt to prepare was full of cheese, fatty meat and full cream. It was lovely for the palate—but not so lovely on my tummy, hips and buns.

While expanding my knowledge of Parisian cuisine—and expanding my inseam in the process—I remembered that a family friend named Tricia Robertson ran culinary tourist trips to the south of France. Called 'A Taste of Provence', her programs included weekend dining and wine tours of country inns and local restaurants. I asked Tricia if I could work as an assistant for her and she agreed to take me on.

While I lived in Provence, I immersed myself in Provençal culture and cooking.

I was surrounded by many amazing culinary artists, and it goes without saying that I was eating as much as I did while in culinary school in London. But I noticed an amazing thing. Despite all this eating and enjoyment of food, my waist size actually went down! I started looked trimmer, slimmer and feeling healthier and more vibrant than I ever had.

It was not for lack of joy in the cooking and eating. Tricia and the local chefs made hearty, scrumptious meals out of the abundant local ingredients. The cuisine emphasised fresh vegetables and fruits, lean meats and seafood.

Tricia's approach to cooking epitomised simple elegance. The recipes were basic, showcasing the natural, mouth-watering flavours of the ingredients themselves, not overcomplicating things or hiding the ingredients in dollops of fat. Olives and olive oil, garlic, chickpeas, onion, tomato, local fish, fennel, sage and other mainstays of Provençal cooking—these became the new colours and flavours with which I painted a healthy eating lifestyle for myself.

More than anything, Tricia taught me the importance of enjoying the process of preparing the food we were eating as well as eating it. Every day we went to the local markets where we were able to touch, feel and smell the ingredients we would put into our bodies only hours later.

The entire process became a sensuous and, dare I say sensual, celebration—a feast not only for the mouth but also for the eyes, nose, hands and soul. Meals were long and lingering and involved indulgent hours of conversation and more than a few glasses of wine.

My body trimmed down while I was enjoying the food I was eating more than ever. My experience in Provence taught me that healthy eating can actually be a pleasure, not a chore. This way of thinking about food has been the essence of my nutritional philosophy ever since.

Food and nutrition really are my number one passion and my work as a nutritionist and chef is based on the cooking skills I learnt in Provence. My recipes use the freshest seasonal ingredients, a little lean meat and lots of vegetarian proteins such as nuts, seeds and legumes, whole grains and very little sugar. I have helped people change the way they eat and achieve optimum health and my clients have all experienced these benefits:

• weight loss
• increased energy
• reduced cravings for sugar and other refined carbohydrates
• more feelings of calm and less stress in their daily lives

And you can too! Food does not need to be the enemy or even a guilty addiction. Healthful eating can be a celebration of life. Let food nourish your body and your soul.

How to Use This Book

If you are reading this book, I imagine that by now you have had experience with other diet books and cookbooks that present eating plans, kilojoule-counting schemes and other rigid formulas for weight loss and health.

However, my own experience goes entirely against this approach to wellness. Kilojoule counting and meal plans would be utterly alien to the way food is approached in Provence. In fact, they go completely against what I learnt there. In Provence, I found balance, health and weight loss simply by eating a particular type of cuisine—one that emphasised fresh vegetables and fruits, lean meats, and direct, sensuous contact with the process of preparing the meals—without a single thought to kilojoule values, rigid schemes or diets.

You don't really need food plans or regimens to achieve the results I did, but I have included some guidelines and eating plans for you to follow if you like. Or you can simply eat meals from this cookbook, and other dishes like them, for breakfast, lunch, dinner and snacks.

☞ Tip

Aim to eat small, healthy meals every 3–4 hours. This will maintain an active metabolism and regulate your blood sugar levels.

Choose the way you want to approach this book:

Dive right in

If you're keen to start cooking and experiencing the health benefits immediately, you can start luxuriating in the simple, elegant, delicious and healthy recipes that follow. All you need to do is eat from the recipes and any others that emphasise fresh fruits and vegetables, whole grains and lean meats.

Read the fine print

Some people appreciate more information and advice, so for you I've included some guidelines in 'Zoe's Twenty Easy Steps to Healthier Eating' (see page 12). These tips will be helpful for anyone seeking a more healthful life and a balanced relationship to food. I include some basic information on reading ingredients labels, ensuring you get enough all-important amino acids in your diet, getting the right kind of sodium, making good fibre choices, snacking on the right foods and eating essential fats.

My way of eating works in part because it radically cuts refined sugar and other refined carbohydrates from your diet. Instead you eat only nutrition-filled fruits and vegetables, complex carbohydrates, healthy fats and lean proteins. The Glycemic Index (see page 24) explains why the food choices I recommend work to restore your body to health, and how to replicate these choices intelligently in the grocery store when deciding what foods to buy.

Get with the program

Read this section if you need advice on how to adopt a more nutritious diet and want to take things slowly. The Six-Week Lifestyle Changing Plan is a program I have developed as a nutritionist and chef that takes you step by step through how to change your eating habits and achieve a healthier lifestyle.

Day-by-day eating plan

Just follow the Simple Seven-day Eating Plan (see page 36) for a week, cooking and eating recipes from the book for breakfast, lunch and dinner. Feel the difference! Then you can make your own weekly planner using different recipes.

Go your own way

After you've cooked some of these dishes and have a feel for your new way of eating, you may want a little more freedom to create your own wonderful meals to achieve phenomenal health and weight results. Try the list of Foods to Avoid and Foods to Have (see page 38), and use the good ingredients in your own recipes.

A new way of eating will introduce you to a whole new range of foods. Turn to the Glossary on page 216 if you're unsure what an ingredient is.

That's it! As you will see from these pages, achieving a healthy, balanced relationship to food, enjoying food instead of fighting it, feeling the energy you've always wanted to feel and achieving the weight loss you've always wanted is really not as difficult as you may have thought.

No-fuss Nutrition

These are the 20 steps I use every day and teach my clients. Health should not be hard work; you just need to make small changes every day and be consistent with those changes.

Twenty Easy Steps to Healthier Eating

1. Aim to lose no more than ½ kilogram (1 pound) of body fat per week, otherwise your basal metabolic rate (BMR) will not be balanced.
2. Measure your body fat percentage at least once a month.
3. Keep a food diary so you can form consistent eating patterns.
4. Your daily fat intake should be 40g; consisting of 30g essential fatty acids (see page 23) and 10g saturated fat, no trans fats.
5. Eat a diet low in saturated fats, animal fat, dairy products, coconut milk, palm oil and ghee, which all increase LDL ('bad' cholesterol)
6. Cut out all trans fatty acids (hydrogenated fats): fried foods, margarines, heated fats and oils, and oils hidden in some biscuits, cakes, bread, muffins, take away foods, dried fruit, muesli and cereals. These all increase LDL (bad cholesterol) and decrease HDL (good cholesterol).
7. Eat a diet high in essential fatty acids (EFAs): fish, avocado, extra virgin olive oil, canola oil, nuts and seeds (raw and unsalted), flaxseed seeds and oil and LSA (a ground mixture of linseed, sunflower seeds and almonds). These increase HDL (good cholesterol) and decrease LDL (bad cholesterol). Aim to eat two servings

of EFAs per day: 1 serving = 1 tablespoon olive, flaxseed or canola oil; 150g (5oz) fish; ¼ cup nuts/seeds (raw and unsalted); a quarter of an avocado; or 1 tablespoon LSA.

8. Cut out simple carbohydrates or high-GI foods: jasmine rice, white flour, sugar, baked goods and most breakfast cereals and breakfast bars.

9. Eat only complex carbohydrates and low-GI foods: fruit, vegetables, wholegrain bread, legumes (lentils, chickpeas, all beans, brown rice, nuts and seeds), spelt or wholemeal pasta and spelt or wholemeal flour.

10. Use the Glycemic Index (see page 204) to help you choose complex carbohydrates. Aim for food with a GI of 50 and below and a fat of 4 and below.

11. Eat protein with each meal and snack. You need 1g per kilogram of body weight of meat protein. For example, if you weigh 69 kilograms (152 pounds), you need 69g of protein. The rest needs to come from vegetarian protein such as grains, vegetables, nuts and seeds.

12. Be wary of marketing and advertising claims such as 'low fat' and 'no fat'. Trust only the nutritional labels on foods and use common sense.

13. See a nutritionist or naturopath to help you with your supplement intake (supplement regime).

14. Don't skip meals. Eat five small meals per day to maintain a high metabolism and regulate your blood sugar levels. Aim to eat every two to three hours.

15. Avoid all fad diets.

16. Drink 2.5 litres (5 pints) of filtered water, herbal teas or fresh vegetable juices per day.

17. Ensure your sodium (salt) intake is only 1g per day.

18. Make sure you are eating at least 40g of fibre every day: psyllium husks, raw fruit, raw vegetables, grains, nuts and seeds.

19. Organisation is the key to good health, so plan what you are going to eat for the week and write a shopping list.

20. Exercise four to five times weekly for a minimum of 30 minutes per day.

Meal-planning Schedule

Aim to eat five to six small meals throughout the day. This will help increase your metabolism and regulate your blood sugar levels.

Before breakfast

- Have two glasses of water with half a fresh lemon, juiced. The body has been in a state of fasting so hydration is most important. The lemon will help stimulate the detoxification process.
- Exercise in the morning or when you can fit it in.

Breakfast

- Eat a balanced breakfast that is a combination of complex carbohydrates, protein and essential fatty acids. Eggs and Soldiers, high-protein breakfast smoothie or the Oat and Amaranth Muesli are all healthy choices.
- Take all of your supplements now.

Snacks: morning and afternoon

- Choose snacks from the Glycemic Index (see page 204) or from the low-GI healthy snacks and juices list (see page 21).
- Eat high-protein snacks such as nuts and seeds, miso soup, vegetable sticks with hummus or cottage cheese, and natural plain yoghurt with LSA and berries. See 'Dips and Snacks' on page 61 for some sexy snack recipes.
- The aim when choosing snacks is to have the low-GI snack (eg. fruit) in the morning and the protein snack in the afternoon. This is because you are more likely to burn the energy contained in the fruit throughout the day. Another reason is that in the afternoon your blood sugar levels may be falling and protein helps stabilise your blood sugar level without causing it to be high and then low, which will create cravings.
- Drink plenty of water.

Lunch

- Eat a meal that is a balance of complex carbohydrates, protein and essential fatty acids.
- Try to eat mainly vegetarian and seafood at lunch.

Dinner

- Again choose a meal that is a balance of complex carbohydrates, protein and essential fatty acids.
- Make sure to eat at least 2–3 hours before going to bed. This will allow the necessary time for the body to detoxify and digest the food.
- Avoid eating too much carbohydrate: eat no more than 1 cup cooked pasta and no more than half to two-thirds of a cup of cooked rice.

After dinner snacks

- If you have a sweet tooth and want a treat after dinner, sip on hot milk or soymilk with honey or a herbal tea.
- Have a small carton of low fat yoghurt.
- Nibble on a handful of unroasted, unsalted nuts and seeds.

Keep it simple:

- Use the Glycemic Index (see page 204)
- Drink 2–3 litres of water per day
- Make sure you eat 2–3 hours before going to bed
- Cut down on carbohydrates late at night
- Rotate your animal protein: red meat, fish, chicken, vegetarian, red meat, fish, vegetarian
- Exercise 30 minutes four to five times a week

How to read labels

Nutrition Information

1. Best before Dec 10
   Chunky Peanut Butter
2. Peanuts (90%), vegetable oil (peanut), salt.
3. Nutrition information

Serving per package: 25g
Serving size: 15g

	Quantity Per serve	Quantity per 100g
Energy	384kj	2560kj
4. Protein	4.4g	20.9g
5. Fat	7.6g	30.7g
saturated	1.5g	11g
trans fats	0.0g	0.0g
6. Carbohydrate		
total	2g	
Sugar	0.9g	6.0g
7. Sodium	1mg	275mg

1. Best before: Check this date for food's freshness.
2. The product's content appears in descending order from the main ingredient, then the second biggest and so on. You'll be able to see what percentage the product's characterising ingredients constitute—so if you're buying peanut butter, you'll know how much of the spread is actually peanuts. Similarly, with yoghurt and jams you'll be able to tell from the label how much real fruit you're getting. If the product contains oil, the label must specify the type of oil—in this case, peanut oil. If you

see hydrogenated or partially hydrogenated fats/oils, it means that they are using trans fatty acids in the product.

3. Nutrition panel: The top section spells out the serving size of the food. Remember that if you double this, you'll double the calorie and fat count, too. The nutrients are listed to show the amount per serve and per 100g (3½ oz or 100ml if liquid). Use the 'per 100g' information to compare similar products. The panel can also help you work out your total nutrient intake for the day and, for example, to check if you're getting enough protein.

4. Protein: You need to have 1g of protein for every kilogram of body weight. For example, 67 kilograms (147 pounds) equals 67g (2oz) of protein per day.

5. Carbohydrates: You need to look at the sugars column, which indicates the amount of sugar that is added to the product. When looking at this column there should never be more than 10g of sugar per 100g (3½ oz) serving of carbohydrates.

6. Fat: Besides spelling out the total fat in a particular food, the nutrition panel must also say how much of it is saturated fat, which is 'bad' fat. This will make it easier to choose brands with the least amount of this fat. The top figure tells you the total in the product. The second figure tells you how much of it is the 'bad' saturated fat. Peanut butter is high in fat but most of it is good fat. If a product is 'low fat' it should have less than 2g fat and a normal product should have no more than about 4g of fat.

7. Sodium: More isn't better when it comes to sodium (see page 20). Your body only needs 2300mg of sodium (one teaspoon) daily. As many products contain too much, it makes sense to check the label. As a guideline: less than 120mg of sodium per 100g (3½ oz) of product is a low sodium content; more than 400mg of sodium per 100g is high; and anything above 1000mg per 100g is very high.

What you want to see on a label

Saturated fat	4g per 100g (3½ oz) normal product, 2g per 100g diet product
Trans fatty acids	Should always be 0g
Sugar	10% = 10g per 100g
Sodium	250mg–300mg per 100g

Eating enough essential amino acids

When we consume proteins, our digestive system breaks them down into amino acids that are the basic building blocks of life. There are 22 naturally occurring amino acids that are divided into two groups: essential and non-essential. The essential amino acids can't be made by our bodies and so must be obtained through our diets. Many foods, such as animal products, contain all the essential amino acids, but other foods contain some but not all. Therefore it becomes necessary to combine certain foods to ensure that all the essential amino acids are present within the body. Essential amino acids, minerals, vitamins and enzymes in the liver make the non-essential amino acids.

Aim to eat protein with every meal and every snack.

Vegetarian Protein Sources

Fruits	Nuts and Seeds	Seaweed
All fruits	Almonds Brazil Cashews Peanuts Pistachios Pumpkin Sesame Sunflower LSA (linseed, sunflower seeds and almonds)	Agar agar Kombu Wakame Kelp Alaria Dulse Nori
Vegetables	**Legumes**	**Micro-Algae**
Carrots Cabbage Cauliflower Broccoli Parsley Brussels sprouts	Azuki beans Dry peas Lentils Soybeans Kidney beans Black beans	Chlorella Spirulina

Grains	Dairy	Ferments
Brown/wild rice	Milk	Soy sauce
Barley	Yoghurt	Tofu
Corn	Cottage cheese	Tamari
Rye	Ricotta	Sourdough bread
Millet	Parmesan	Nut/seed yoghurt
Buckwheat	Feta	Miso tempeh
Oats	Goats cheese	Soya mince
Amaranth	Mozzarella	
Quinoa	Eggs (no more than 4 per week)	
Wild rice		
Bulgar		
Whole wheat		
Wheatgerm		
Yeast		

What is the best source of sodium?

Sodium is necessary for maintaining proper water balance and blood pH. It is needed for stomach, nerve and muscle function. Sodium deficiency is rare as most people have adequate (if not excessive) levels of sodium in their bodies. Virtually all foods contain sodium. Choosing the right source is your answer to a proper balance of health.

A bad source of sodium is mostly found in refined and processed foods. Also refining and processing removes many needed minerals, trace minerals and vitamins from foods. Not only are additives and chemicals (sodium being one them) incapable of supporting life themselves, when combined with fresh foods the food itself is chemically changed and the fresh food's original state is diminished.

In addition, micro-organisms and bacteria can develop resistance to ion radiation and other preservatives so that food can still appear edible when it is seriously contaminated. So avoiding these types of foods will not only increase your health but reduce the amount of negative sodium you would be ingesting.

Salt substitutes

- Mineral salts and seasonings: Celtic salts, robust kelp, sea vegetables, sea salt and herb mix. Use to taste.
- Herbal seasonings: these have no or very little sodium. Use to taste.
- Miso: use to taste in casseroles, gravies, soups and sauces; a little goes a long way.
- Bragg Liquid Amino: pure vegetable amino acids; use to taste in any dish needing more salt.
- Spices and citrus zests: use one or more to taste in place of salt in sweet or savoury recipes.
- Tamari: low in sodium and wheat free; a much better choice than regular soy sauce.

High-protein and low-GI healthy snacks and juices

Choose snacks that are low in refined carbohydrates and high in protein. This will help keep you feeling satisfied and will help stabilise your blood sugar and reduce cravings and overeating. Remember, a snack is not a mini-meal, so don't overeat.

- Curried egg dip with carrot sticks
- Soy milk or skim milk smoothie with fruit (no ice-cream or sweet yoghurt)
- Cucumber, mint and yoghurt dip with multigrain toasted bread cut into squares
- Fruit frappe: frozen berries, banana and fresh juice
- Fruit: apple, pear, apricot, banana, half a mango, 1 cup grapes, grapefruit, 1 small wedge of rockmelon or 20 cherries

- Marinated tofu cubes and cherry tomato skewers
- Unsalted and raw nuts: almonds, walnuts, chestnuts, cashews, pecans, macadamias, pine nuts, sunflower seeds and pepitas (no more than a quarter cup per day)
- Raw vegetable sticks with homemade Carrot, Coriander and Cottage Cheese Dip
- 1 piece of soy and linseed bread with tomato and Asian Salmon Dip
- 1 cup homemade vegetable soup
- Natural plain yoghurt with fruit, berries and/or flaxseed
- Soy yoghurt (unsweetened)
- 1 slice of fruit loaf (non-commercial brand)
- Baked beans (salt reduced) from the health food store
- Popcorn: no butter or salt
- Muesli bar (non-commercial brand)
- 2 small Fish Balls with coriander and chilli dipping sauce
- Dried apricots, plums, apple, pear or peach: no more than a third of a cup per day, always organic as they don't contain sulphur dioxides
- 50g wedge of ricotta with honey on wholegrain bread (soy and linseed or pumpernickel)
- 1x30g rice cake with low fat ricotta and half a banana
- 1 slice of soy and linseed bread with health nut spread: from the health food shop
- Tomato, avocado and vegemite on soy and linseed bread
- Hard-boiled egg with chilli sea salt and soldiers: wholegrain toast
- Fruit salad with low fat natural plain yoghurt
- Small tin of tuna, salmon or sardines

Juicing is a fantastic way to increase vitamins and minerals into your daily food intake and it is an excellent detox. When choosing a juice try to make it two-thirds vegetable and one-third fruit. This way it will reduce the fructose (fruit sugars) in your diet.

- Apple and aloe vera: great for the bowel
- Apple, carrot, spinach, beetroot, parsley and ginger: iron booster
- Apple, lime and mint: flat tummy juice
- Beetroot, carrot, celery, tomato and parsley, spirulina: detox juice
- Carrot, beetroot, spinach and lemon: stress buster
- Beetroot, carrot and spinach: blood cleanser
- Spinach, pear, apple and ginger: energiser
- Spinach, beetroot, lemon, parsley: drink that cellulite away
- Apple, ginger, lime and orange: stimulator
- Parsley, honeydew melon, carrots and ginger: skin cleanser
- Chilled lemon, honey and water: soothes sore throats
- Pink grapefruit, lemon, lime and orange: tangy and good for the liver

What are essential fatty acids?

Eating fat is essential for health. In the past few years, researchers have begun to understand the fundamental role that essential fatty acids (EFAs) play in health and wellness. Without these EFAs, life would not exist.

EFAs are called essential because the body needs them but cannot produce them on its own. Essential fatty acids must come from our diet. There are two types of EFAs, both of which are especially important to cardiovascular health: alpha-linolenic acid (omega-3 fatty acid) and linoleic acid (omega-6 fatty acid). The current Western diet includes too much omega-6 fatty acids because the refining process used for commercial oils has removed nearly all omega-3 fatty acids.

You need to include omega-3 and unprocessed omega-6 EFAs in each of your meals. Flaxseed, sesame, sunflower and wheatgerm oils, extra virgin olive oil, avocado, LSA and fish (in capsule, meal or liquid form) are all great sources of EFAs.

Essential fatty acids can help to reduce blood pressure and blood cholesterol, help muscle tissue recuperate, lubricate the joints, reduce triglycerides, and even reduce pain and inflammation caused by arthritis.

The importance of fibre

Fibre plays a vital role in maintaining good health that can be filled by no other substance in our diet. Fibre can be divided into two classes, each with a different role in health: soluble fibre and insoluble fibre. Taken together they are called Total Dietary Fibre. The recommendations for Total Dietary Fibre vary between 35–50g (about 1½oz) per day. In most Western cultures, people eat only 8–10 grams. Soluble fibre is found in foods such as oats, apples, beans and pears, while insoluble fibre is found in whole grains, peas and corn.

Fibre has many health benefits—and the list is growing. One of the benefits of a high fibre diet is the decreased incidence of colon cancer. Fibre also helps to halt constipation and lower cholesterol levels (possibly lowering the risk of heart disease).

Fibre can help diabetics by controlling the rate at which carbohydrates are absorbed into the bloodstream, reducing insulin spikes.

Unlike simple sugars, fats and proteins, fibre is the part of our food from plant sources that we are unable to digest. It does not produce energy or build body tissue; it passes through to the large intestine virtually unchanged, therefore contains no calories.

The Glycemic Index

Back in the 1800s, sugar made up only 10 per cent of people's diets. Today, 60 per cent of most people's diet is sugar. Sugar is now being found to be a major cause of diabetes, low energy levels, excess body fat and cellulite and decreased athletic performance. Sugar is not just an empty kilojoule that has no nutritional value; it destroys the neurological pathways of the central nervous system (CNS).

The glycemic index (GI) is a ranking of foods based on their overall effects on blood sugar levels. This index measures how much blood sugar increases in the two or three hours after eating. A low GI (60 and below) means a smaller rise of blood sugar levels. A high GI (above 60) means a larger rise in blood sugar levels.

The glycemic index is about foods high in carbohydrates. A lot of people still think that it is plain table sugar that people with diabetes need to avoid. The experts used to say that, but the glycemic index shows that even complex carbohydrates such as baked potatoes can be even worse.

When you make use of the glycemic index to prepare healthy meals, it helps to keep your blood sugar levels under control. This will increase your energy levels, speed up the process of weight loss and increase athletic performance.

The speed of digestion and absorption of foods are rated in comparison to glucose (a sugar), which has a glycemic index of 137. The following list is a compiled list of foods tested to date.

Foods 70 and up are considered high, 50–69 moderate, and those below 50 are considered low. It is recommended that you totally avoid the foods that are rated 70 and up and choose foods that are rated under 60. For a list of the GI rating of common foods, see page 204.

Six-week Lifestyle Changing Plan

If you're aiming to make changes to your diet or lifestyle, it's important that you do it progressively. Making a couple of changes each week will still drastically reduce the amount of kilojoules in your diet. You will never succeed if you try to change everything at once because it won't be sustainable in relation to your lifestyle.

Start by keeping a food diary, writing down everything you eat and drink, any exercise you do and any areas you feel you need to change. For example, do you pig out when you come home from work or when you watch television after dinner? Writing down what you do now will help to highlight areas that need improving. Keep writing in your food diary for the entire six weeks. It's a proven fact that people who keep a food diary lose weight. No cheating!

During the six-week program you need to:
- Keep a food diary
- Eat three normal meals and two or three healthy snacks throughout the day. Eating every two or three hours helps increase your metabolism and balance your blood sugar levels
- Drink 2–3 litres (68–101fl oz) of water per day, no more than 200ml (7fl oz) at a time
- Exercise a minimum of three times a week for 30 minutes each time

Eating from all the food groups

A healthy diet includes all the three main food groups in each meal. Your body will get all the nutrients it requires, which means your cravings decrease and you lose weight.

EFAs	Complex	Protein: Animal and Vegetable
Avocado	Brown long grain rice	Fish
All fish	Whole grains	Chicken
Raw and unsalted nuts almonds, cashews, walnuts	All beans	Red meat
Extra virgin olive oil (unheated)	All peas	Dairy
Flaxseed oil	Multigrain or wholemeal bread	Lentils
Canola oil	All vegetable	All beans
Raw and unsalted seeds, sunflower seeds, pepitas, sesame seeds	All fruits	All nuts
Wheatgerm oil	Lentils	All seeds
		All grains: quinoa, amaranth, barley, buckwheat
		Tofu

Week 1: Eat a healthy breakfast and drink more water. Eat other meals as normal.

Breakfast

Start with your breakfast. Breakfast needs to be eaten at home as this will help to break the fast and will initiate your metabolism, increasing kilojoule burning throughout the day. You need to aim to eat a snack mid-morning and mid-afternoon. Frequent small meals spread over the day will help to maintain your metabolism and will stop your blood sugar levels falling. A side effect of not eating breakfast is cravings and energy lows.

Breakfast ideas

On one to two slices of multigrain bread:

- Banana
- Avocado and tomato
- Cottage cheese and mushrooms
- Feta cheese and tomato
- Asian Salmon Dip
- Spiced Hummus with sliced tomatoes
- High-protein Fruit Smoothie

Cereals:

Medium-size bowl of approximately ½ to 1 cup of cereal with low-fat milk.

- Porridge (not instant, but traditional oats) with fresh berries
- Untoasted muesli with fresh fruit
- High-protein muesli
- Natural plain yoghurt with fresh fruit
- Fruity Bircher Muesli
- Oat and Amaranth Muesli
- Raw Berry Porridge

Cooked breakfast:
- Poached eggs with tomato on full-grain bread
- Scrambled eggs with one full egg and one egg white
- Small tin of salt-reduced baked beans
- Omelette with 1 full egg and 1 egg white, Spanish (red) onion and herbs.
- Eggs and Soldiers
- High-protein Omelette
- Poached Eggs with Ham
- Scrambled Tofu

Liquids

Water really is the essence of life and it will definitely help with weight loss. Eliminating drinks like soft drinks, fruit juices, coffee, tea and alcohol will drastically cut calories from your diet. The body requires 2.4 litres (5 pints) of fluids per day. This can come from water, herbal teas and fresh vegetable juice (not bottled fruit juice because of the high calories). Keep a 1.5 litre (3 pint) bottle of water on your desk and progressively sip all day (no more than 200ml (7fl oz) at a time).

Liquid alternatives:
- Water
- Freshly squeezed vegetable juices (see 'low-GI snacks and juices' on page 21)
- Herbal teas: green tea, dandelion tea (fantastic for the liver), chamomile tea, liquorice tea (excellent if you have a sugar craving)

Week 2: Include 2–3 healthy snacks, focus on organisation and reduce takeaway foods and eating out

Organisation is the key to success. Write a shopping list at the beginning of the week (or use the shopping list provided), which includes ingredients for breakfast, lunch, dinner and snacks for the week. Keep all your healthy snacks at work so you do not have the temptation to go to the shop for a quick muffin or coffee or reach for the 3pm chocolate bar.

The focus for this week, apart from organisation and snacks, is reducing the amount of takeaway and restaurant food you consume. These contain a high amount of empty kilojoules and often have unnecessary and unrealistic portion sizes. Allow yourself one cheat day a week.

Snack ideas

- Fresh fruit
- Low-GI dried fruit eg. apple, prunes, figs, apricots
- Unsalted and unroasted nuts and seeds (cashews, almonds, hazelnuts, sunflower seeds, pumpkins seeds. NO peanuts)
- Fresh vegetables cut up with hummus, tzatziki or a quarter of an avocado with lemon juice
- High-protein Fruit Smoothie
- Freshly squeezed vegetable juices
- 1 rye crispbread with tomato and cottage cheese and a little pepper to taste
- 1 piece of multigrain bread with a banana and low fat ricotta
- Bean and Rosemary Dip with 1 rice cake
- Natural plain yoghurt
- Marinated tofu cubes and cherry tomato skewers
- Asian Salmon Dip on 1 slice of multigrain bread
- Cucumber, mint and yoghurt dip with carrot and red pepper sticks
- Chickpea and Carrot Dip with celery sticks
- Hard Boiled Egg with sea salt and chilli

Week 3: Reduce simple carbohydrates, increase complex carbohydrates and eat a healthy lunch

Simple carbohydrates (white bread, flour, rice, baked goods, sugar and honey) convert to glucose rapidly, causing your blood sugar levels to rise very quickly then fall. This means that the body will have an excess of glucose that needs to be burnt. If it is not burnt it is converted into fat. It will also play havoc with your energy levels, causing mid-morning and mid-afternoon lows. This will increase sugar cravings.

Increase your lunch-time consumption of complex carbohydrates such as full-grain bread, basmati or brown rice, wholemeal or spelt pasta, fruit, vegetables, legumes, nuts and seeds. These are converted into glucose much slower than simple carbohydrates. This means they will fill you up for longer and you will eat less. Complex carbohydrates also have the effect of maintaining higher energy levels.

The Glycemic Index (see page 204) will help you choose carbohydrates wisely.

Lunch ideas
- Vegetable soups
- 1 small tin of tuna, salmon or sardines on full-grain bread and salad
- Wholemeal pita bread wrap with chicken, avocado salad and using hummus as a spread
- Small serving of tomato-based pasta with a green salad
- Stir-fry vegetables with basmati or brown rice.
- Mixed bean salad with feta, tomato, avocado and a dressing of olive oil and lemon juice or balsamic and olive oil
- BBQ Lamb Skewers with yoghurt dipping sauce and a small salad
- Cauliflower and Almond Salad
- Curried Sweet Potato Soup (no bread)
- Easy Vegetable and Chicken Curry (no rice)

Week 4: Eat a healthy dinner, reduce saturated fats from your diet and increase essential fatty acids

Aim to have a healthy dinner two to three hours before going to bed. This will help with digestion, sleep and liver function. If you are time-poor or you are getting home very late, try having your main meal at lunch time and a lighter meal such as soup at dinner time. This will ensure you do not overeat at night.

Eliminate high saturated fatty meats from your diet. Try grilling, steaming or oven roasting chicken or fish instead of frying. Try tuna, salmon or sardines rather than a roast beef sandwich. Cut out fats such as mayonnaise, cheese and butter. Increase your intake of essential fatty acids (EFAs) or omega-3 fats. See 'What are essential fatty acids (EFAs)?' on page 230. Eat two servings of EFAs per day. Examples of one serve are: one tablespoon of olive oil, canola oil or flaxseed oil; 150g (5oz) fish; ¼ cup nuts and seeds; or ¼ avocado.

Dinner ideas

- The best dinner to have is lean fish, chicken or meat with a selection of vegetable and/or salad
- Grilled fish with a mixed bean salad and steamed carrots sprinkled with sesame seeds
- Roasted chicken with roasted sweet potato (yam), carrots and beetroot with green salad
- Vegetable frittata with a rocket and avocado salad
- Chicken patties with a green salad
- Asian Stir-fry with Tuna and brown or basmati rice
- Turkey and Vegetable Soup with 1 piece of full-grain bread
- Eye Fillet with Walnut and Rosemary Quinoa
- Grilled Tuna with Ligurian Olive and Basil Tapenade
- Chicken and Vegetable Millet Pilaf
- Prawn and Avocado Salad

Week 5: Reduce and manage your portion sizes and focus on eating daily nutrition requirements

Portion sizes are very important. Most people overeat by up to 30 per cent each day so aim to eat 30 per cent less than what you are currently eating and always leave a little food on your plate, if it is appropriate.

A good way to reduce your portions without feeling like you are starving yourself is to reduce all your main meals by 30 per cent and have it as a snack about an hour later. Use your palm as an indicator of how much meat, chicken or fish to eat. Meat is a palm size and palm width; chicken is to the first knuckle and palm width; and fish the whole hand size and total width.

General portion amounts and daily requirements

- 4–5 servings of vegetable (1 serving = ½ cup of most vegetables or 1 cup of lettuce or spinach)
- 2–3 servings of fruit (1 serving = ½ cup of fruit)
- 2 servings of EFAs (1 serving = 1 tablespoon olive oil, flaxseed oil or canola oil; 150g (5oz) fish; ¼ cup raw and unsalted nuts and seeds; ¼ avocado)
- 3–4 servings of complex carbohydrates (1 serving = ½ cup of brown rice, 1 cup cooked pasta; 1–2 servings bread = 1 piece of bread; 1 serving of grains = ½ cup of grains)
- 1 serving of animal protein (1 serving = 150g (5oz))
- 2–3 servings of vegetable protein each day (1 serving = ½ cup)

Meal examples
Example 1
Breakfast:	A bowl of rolled oats, unprocessed bran, and water or; 2 pieces of soy and linseed bread with low sugar jam, prune spread or very good quality jam or; mashed banana with ricotta. Herbal tea.
Morning tea:	¼ cup mixed nuts (raw and unsalted) such as almonds, pepitas, sunflower seeds and raw cashews.
Lunch:	A large container of mixed salad with tofu or mixed beans. 2–3 pieces of fruit, banana, pears, green apples or pineapple
Afternoon tea:	Natural plain yoghurt with strawberries. Herbal tea.
Dinner:	A big plate of steamed vegetables with brown rice or wholemeal pasta served with a good quality homemade tomato sauce. When having meats, keep to fish or chicken to lower the saturated fats.
Dessert:	Another small bowl of porridge or a fruit salad with 3 tablespoons of plain yoghurt (goat, cow, sheep or soy yoghurt) and 1 tablespoon LSA.

Example 2
Breakfast:	1-2 Eggs and Soldiers
Morning tea:	Asian Salmon Dip with vegetable sticks
Lunch:	Lentil and Spinach Soup Chicken and Vegetable Patties with a small salad
Afternoon tea:	Hard Boiled Egg with Sea Salt and Chilli
Dinner:	Mediterranean Lamb Burgers with Guilt-free Mashed Potatoes
Dessert:	Toasted Nuts with Strawberry Puree and Yoghurt

Week 6: Making habits permanent and adopting a healthy mental approach to eating

The main aim of following the Six-week Lifestyle Changing Plan is to establish permanent new habits. If you focus on weight loss you will do anything to lose weight, such as starving yourself or exercising until you practically pass out. But if you focus on diet and exercise you will lose weight in a healthy way, and you will make these changes your new habits.

Make a list of all the areas you would still like to improve and jot down things you've got better at. For example, 'I haven't skipped breakfast for six weeks', or 'I need to drink more water'.

Stay positive and don't be too hard on yourself. A sure way to stop eating the correct food is to berate yourself or put yourself down. Whenever my habits fly out the window I let them go and actually enjoy having a meal off. What I then do is use the next meal to reduce my kilojoule consumption—it's all about balance!

Simple Seven-day Eating Plan

	Monday	Tuesday
Breakfast	High-protein Omelette (p. 51) with 2 eggs, (no bread)	High-protein Fruit Smoothie (p. 47)
Morning snack	¼ cup of raw and unsalted nuts	Curried Egg Dip
Lunch	Beef and Vegetable Soup (p. 87) served with a salad	Raw Salad with Tuna Agave and Avocado Dressing (p. 115) vegetable and
Afternoon snack	Cucumber, mint and yoghurt dip with carrot sticks	Marinated Tofu and Cherry Tomato Skewers
Dinner	Asian Stir-fry with Tuna (p. 147) or tofu and vegetables with a sauce using ginger, garlic, tamari soy and chili	Grilled Miso Chicken (p. 157) served with minimum 1 cup steamed vegetables
After dinner snack	Toasted Nuts with Strawberry Puree and Yoghurt	Hot milk with Honey and Cinnamon

Wednesday	Thursday	Friday	Saturday	Sunday
High-protein Scrambled Eggs (p. 52) on 1 slice multigrain bread	Fruity Bircher Muesli (p. 45)	Scrambled Tofu (p. 55)-on 1 slice multigrain bread	Eggs and Soldiers (p. 44)	Raw Berry Porridge (p. 56)
Asian Salmon Dip with 1 slice of multigrain bread	Fresh fruit with natural yoghurt	Energiser Juice	Chickpea and carrot dip with celery sticks	Carrot, Coriander (Cilantro) and Cottage Cheese Dip with Vegetable Sticks
Chicken Breast with Raw Tomato and Red Capsicum Sauce (p. 93)	Lentil and Spinach Soup (p. 106) served with a garden salad	Tuna and Zucchini Frittata (p. 133) served with a tomato and basil salad	Chicken and Vegetable Patties (p. 91) served with steamed vegetables	Wild Mushroom Soup (p. 124) served with a garden salad
Tangy and good-for-the-liver juice	Healthy Tuna Dip	Bean and Rosemary Dip with celery sticks	Hard Boiled Egg with Sea Salt and Chilli	Drink-that-cellulite-away juice
Beef, Tomato and Pea Curry (p. 153) served with steamed vegetables	Prawn and Avocado Salad (p.178) in a lettuce cup	Lactose-free Chicken Boscaiola (p. 168) served with a green salad	Citrus Marinated Salmon with Vegetable Salad (p. 159)	Chicken Breast with Roast Vegetables (p. 156)
Herbal tea with a little honey and mint	Natural unsweetened yoghurt	10 almonds with half an apple	Roasted Coconut and Spring Fruit Salad	Carob Delight Cookies

Good Foods, Bad Foods

So often when it comes to changing our diet we have a massive NO list and a very small YES list, which can be very intimidating. Below is a general guideline of the foods you should aim to eat less in your diet and the foods that should make up the majority of your diet.

Food to have

Breads and wraps
All multigrain breads and wraps 1-2 slices per day

Dairy and alternatives
Low-fat yoghurt
Low-fat or skimmed milk
Cottage cheese
Goat's cheese
Eggs (free range) 2–4 per week
Rice milk
Soy milk
Tofu or tempeh

Fats
Extra virgin olive oil
Flaxseed oil
Sunflower oil
Borage oil
Sesame seed oil

Grains and Nuts
All nuts as long as they are unroasted and unsalted
All grains

Legumes

Black beans
Soybeans
Kidney beans
Pinto beans
Chickpeas
Lentils
Navy beans

Fruit

All berries
Apricots
Apples
All citrus fruits
Pears
Peaches
Plums
Nectarines
Avocado
Tomato

Meats

All seafood
Skinless chicken and turkey breast
Lean red meat 150g 1–2 per week
Lean pork 150g 1–2 per week

Pasta

Wholewheat pasta
Spelt pasta
Soy pasta
Rice noodles

Seasonings

Any herbs, fresh or dried
Liquid Amino by Bragg
Sea salt or Celtic salt

Vegetables

All and any vegetables

Foods to avoid

Bread and grains

Refined white flour products
Wheat gluten
Waffles
White bagels
Cornflakes
Popped rice
Any refined cereals
Toasted muesli
Sweet processed biscuits
White processed pasta or noodles

Dairy foods

Coloured, hard cheese
Ice-cream
Full-fat milk
Butter and margarines

Drinks

Carbonated soda
Coffee (maximum 2–3 per week)
Alcohol (try to either limit to 1–2 standard
drinks per night or drink every alternate
day. Drink a maxiumum of ten units of
alcohol per week. 1 unit of wine = 100ml,
30ml nip of spirits or a middy of beer)
Caffeinated drinks
Processed fruit juices

Fats

All hydrogenated oils or trans fatty acids

Meats

Bacon
Hot dogs
Sausages
Salami
Luncheon meats
Meatloaf

Others

Artificial sweeteners
Fried foods
Fermented foods
Refined and processed foods, chips, chocolate, hard candy, junk foods, etc
Foods containing artificial colouring or flavouring or preservatives
Manufactured foods
Salt
Food actives BHA and BHT

Sauces

Tomato sauce
Soy sauce (tamari is suitable)
Commercial mayonnaise
Sweet chilli sauce

Sugars

Glucose
Maltose
Refined sugar (white and brown)

☞ Tip

Exercise is so important for keeping the body feeling healthy and energised. When we exercise we release hormones such as serotonin, which is helpful in inducing sleep.

Fruity Bircher Muesli (see next page

Breakfast

Breakfast really is the most important meal of the day. Not only will it help break the fast, it will give your metabolism the boost it needs to give you the energy to start the day. So often we choose high carbohydrate breakfasts that elevate blood sugar levels and then cause them to crash, leaving you craving more carbohydrates or lacking in energy, which so often causes you to eat or drink something sweet or coffee. Eating a healthy combination of complex carbohydrate and protein in all your breakfast meals with help stop the craving and will help you feel more satiated.

All the breakfast recipes are quick, easy and above all nutritious, exactly what you want in the morning.

Eggs and Soldiers

Prep time: 10–15 minutes

Serves: 2

Utensils:
Eggcups
Saucepan
Serving plate

2 whole eggs
Multigrain bread for toasting
Salt and pepper for seasoning

Place the eggs in a saucepan and cover with water. Turn on a high heat and once the water is boiling cook for 2 minutes.

Place the cooked eggs in eggcups with the cooked toast cut into strips lengthways. Season and eat.

☞ Tip

Balance your sodium intake to 1g per day. Use products such as sea salt, herb salt, tamari soy sauce or miso paste as alternatives for salt.

½–1 cup oats (soaked overnight if needed)
1 tablespoon organic currants
1 apple or firm pear
½ lemon or orange
2 tablespoons natural plain yoghurt
1 teaspoon honey
1 tablespoon mixed nuts and seeds (almonds, flaxseed, sunflower seeds or LSA)
A pinch of cinnamon or fresh ginger powder

Soak the oats with the currants the night before or for an hour in a little water or fruit juice.

Combine grated apple or pear with a squeeze of lemon juice and one or two tablespoons of natural plain yoghurt.

Drizzle with honey and sprinkle with chopped nuts and cinnamon or ginger.

This recipe uses apple or pear, but you can use almost any other fruit. Add sliced or mashed banana, or a handful of fresh berries, or some chopped dried fruit such as apricots, dates, figs, pears, sultanas or raisins to change the flavour.

Fruity Bircher Muesli

Prep time: 7–15 minutes
Serves: 1

Utensils:
Grater
Measuring cups
Large mixing bowl
Juicer

High-protein Fruit Smoothie

1 cup skim, soy, oat, rice or cows milk
1 cup water
½ cup mixed berries, fresh or frozen
2 tablespoons low fat natural plain yoghurt
2 tablespoons oats
1 tablespoon psyllium
1 scoop whey protein powder
1 teaspoon cinnamon
4 ice cubes

Place all the ingredients in a food processor or blender and blend until thoroughly mixed. Serve in a chilled glass.

Prep time: 5–10 minutes
Serves: 1

Utensils:
Food processor
Chilled glass

High-protein Soy Yoghurt Drink

Prep time: 10–15 minutes
Serves: 1 people

Utensils:
Food processor
Chilled glass

1 cup low fat plain soy yoghurt
½ cup silken tofu
1 tablespoon lecithin
1 scoop soy protein powder (optional)
1 pear, core removed
1 teaspoon nutmeg

Place the ingredients into blender and blend until smooth. Serve in a chilled glass.

☞ Tip

If your little one is feeling low, try giving them a mango smoothie. They are high in vitamin A and E and are even said to help with depression!

High-protein Muesli

5 cups rolled oats
2 cups of puffed amaranth
1 cup oat bran
¼ cup pepitas
¼ cup sunflower seeds
¼ cup LSA or flaxseeds, ground
½ cup psyllium husks

Combine all ingredients in a large bowl and mix together and store in an airtight container. Place ¾ of a cup in a bowl with 1–2 tablespoons low fat plain natural yoghurt and either soy milk or light cow's milk. Sprinkle protein powder over the top if desired.

Prep time: 10 minutes
Serves: 10–12

Utensils:
Large mixing bowl
Measuring cups
Measuring spoons
Serving bowl

2 whole eggs
2 tablespoons cottage cheese
¼ Spanish (red) onion, finely chopped
¼ tomato, finely chopped
2 button mushrooms, finely chopped
1 tablespoon fresh or dried basil
Salt and pepper to season
1–2 teaspoons olive oil for the frying pan

Crack the eggs in a bowl and whisk until light and fluffy. Place all the other in the bowl and mix thoroughly.
Place a frying plan on a medium heat with a little olive oil. Place all the omelette mixture into the pan and leave for 3–5 minutes and until cooked through. With a spatula, flip half of the omelette onto the other half and tip onto a plate. Serve on its own with a little salt and pepper to taste.

High-protein Omelette

Prep time: 10–15 minutes
Serves: 1

Utensils:
Mixing bowl
Sharp knife
Whisk
Frying pan
Spatula

High-protein Scrambled Eggs with Cottage Cheese

Prep time: 10–15 minutes
Serves: 1

Utensils:
Mixing bowl
Sharp knife
Whisk
Frying pan
Spatula

2 whole eggs
2 tablespoons cottage cheese
¼ Spanish (red) onion, finely chopped
¼ tomato, finely chopped
2 button mushrooms, finely chopped
1 tablespoon fresh or dried basil
Salt and pepper to season
1–2 teaspoons olive oil for the frying pan

Crack the eggs in a bowl and whisk until light and fluffy. Place all the other ingredients in the bowl and mix thoroughly.
Place a frying plan on medium heat with a little olive oil. Place the entire mixture into the pan and mix with a spoon until cooked.
Serve on its own or with multigrain bread with a little salt and pepper to taste.

Oat and Amaranth Muesli

250g (8oz) oats
250g (8oz) puffed amaranth
100g (3½oz) organic apricots cut into quarters
100g (3½oz) organic apples cut into quarters
50g (1¾oz) pepitas
50g (1¾oz) sesame seeds
1 teaspoon cinnamon

To serve:
1–2 tablespoons sheep's milk yoghurt
1 tablespoon LSA
1–2 teaspoons honey

Place all ingredients into a mixing bowl and mix thoroughly. Serve approximately 1 cup of muesli with 1–2 tablespoons sheep's milk yoghurt, LSA and honey

Prep time: 15–20 minutes
Serves: 4

Utensils:
Mixing bowl
Measuring scales
Small bowls for the ingredients
Small serving bowls
Measuring spoons

☞ Tip

To avoid a hangover, drink a litre of water as soon as your arrive home and take a vitamin B supplement. The Vitamin B helps your body process the alcohol and metabolise the carbohydrates

Poached Eggs with Ham

Prep time: 10 minutes
Serves: 1

Utensils:
Saucepan or frying pan
Slotted spoon
Serving plate

1 whole egg
50g (1¾oz) good quality ham off the bone
1 tablespoon vinegar for poaching water
Salt and pepper to season
1 slice of multigrain bread

Place water and vinegar in a saucepan or a frying pan and boil. Crack the egg into the boiled water without breaking the yolk. It will take 2–3 minutes to cook. With a slotted spoon remove the poached egg and plate on a paper towel and remove the excess water.

Toast your bread and then serve it on a plate with the ham and then the egg on top. Season with salt and pepper.

☞ Tip

Drink no more than 1 cup of coffee or 2 cups of tea per day. Try drinking chamomile tea before sleeping. It is very calming and contains no caffeine.

¼ Spanish (red) onion
¼ cup mushrooms
¼ cup cherry tomato, chopped in halves
1 cup organic hard tofu, crumbled
1 garlic clove, crushed
Small handful of basil or flat leaf parsley
½ teaspoon fresh chilli

Sauté the Spanish onion, garlic, mushrooms and tomatoes in a frying pan for about 5 minutes. Add the tofu, chilli and basil into the saucepan with the onion mixture and cook until heated through; approximately 7 minutes.
Serve with a drizzle of extra virgin olive oil and season.

Scrambled Tofu

Prep time: 15–17 minutes
Serves: 2

Utensils:
Frying pan
Measuring cups
Measuring spoons
Garlic crusher
Serving plate

Raw Berry Porridge

Prep time: 10 minutes
Serves: 1

Utensils:
Food processor
Serving glass or bowl

1 cup milk
1 cup rolled oats
1 tablespoon psyllium husks
1 cup berries
½ banana
1 scoop whey protein powder (optional)

Place all the ingredients into a food processor and blend until smooth. Serve in either a bowl or glass.

Vegetable and Cottage Cheese Scrambled Eggs

Prep time: 10–15 minutes
Serves: 2

Utensils:
Mixing bowl
Sharp knife
Whisk
Frying pan

4 egg whites
4 tablespoons of cottage cheese
¼ cup mushrooms, finely sliced
¼ cup red capsicum, finely chopped
¼ cup baby spinach, roughly chopped
1 tablespoon fresh parsley, finely chopped
Salt and pepper to season
1–2 teaspoons olive oil for the frying pan

Crack the eggs in a bowl and whisk until light and fluffy. Place all the other ingredients in the bowl and mix thoroughly.

Place a frying plan on a medium heat with a little olive oil. Pour the mixture into the pan and stir until cooked.

Serve with a quartered tomato or a salad.

Dips and Snacks

We have been told not to snack so often people are scared of snacking. Snacking is a fantastic way to help stabilise your blood sugar levels and stopped the morning and afternoon cravings. It is also helps you to stop you overeat in your main meals. But it all comes down to what you snack on. My recipes are all yummy and healthy, guilt free snacks. Keep in mind that snacks are not meant to be mini-meals so keep within the portions suggested in the recipes.

Asian Salmon Dip

Prep time: 15 minutes
Serves: 6

Utensils:
Mixing bowl
Grater
Sharp knife
Squeezer

100g (3½oz) tin salmon in spring water
1 tablespoon reduced-salt soy sauce or tamari
1 teaspoon finely grated fresh ginger
1 tablespoon finely chopped fresh mint
1 tablespoon finely chopped coriander (cilantro)
1 teaspoon lime juice
1 tablespoon orange juice
½ teaspoon finely chopped fresh chilli (remove seeds to reduce heat)

Place all the ingredients into a mixing bowl and mix thoroughly.

Serve with a selection of freshly chopped vegetable sticks. Try baby corn for something different.

☞ Tip

Try to avoid chips and savoury biscuits. Try raw and unsalted nuts or pepitas instead. Nuts are a fantastic source of essential fatty acids and are high in protein..

Chickpea and Carrot Dip

1 x 400g (14oz) tin chickpeas, rinsed and drained
1 teaspoon paprika
1 teaspoon cumin
1 tablespoon lemon juice
½ teaspoons honey or agave nectar
1 large carrot, peeled and grated
1 large cucumber cut into 1cm (½in) rounds

Place chickpeas in a blender or food processor.
Add paprika, cumin, lemon juice and honey or
agave nectar, and puree until smooth.
Stir grated carrot through the chickpea mixture.
Spoon onto cucumber rounds and serve.

Prep time: 15 minutes
Makes 30 pieces

Utensils:
Blender
Juicer
Mixing bowls
Spoons

Bean and Rosemary Dip

1 cup dried white beans
1 cup homemade or very good quality chicken or
vegetable stock
2 garlic gloves, chopped
Juice of 1 lemon
Salt and pepper to season
1 tablespoon chopped rosemary leaves

Put the beans in a large bowl, cover with water and soak for several hours or until soft. Drain and rinse under cold water. Put the beans in a saucepan and cover with water. Cover and bring to a boil, reduce heat and simmer for 1 hour. When ready, they should be tender but still hold their shape. Blend the beans and any remaining liquid in a food processor.
Heat ¼ cup stock in a saucepan. Add the garlic and rosemary and cook for 2 minutes. Add the bean puree and mix well. Add remaining stock and cook for 10 minutes until the mixture is smooth and thick. Remove from heat and cool.
Add the lemon juice, and season with salt and fresh pepper to taste. Mix well.
Spoon into a serving bowl and garnish with the rosemary. Serve with soy and linseed toast soldiers or carrot and celery sticks.

Prep time: 15 minutes
Serves: 6

Utensils:
Soaking bowl
Saucepan
Measuring spoons
Juicer
Measuring cups
Serving bowl

Hard-boiled Eggs with Sea Salt and Chilli Mix

Prep time: 10 minutes
Serves: 1

Utensils:
Small mixing bowl
Sharp knife
Serving plate

1–2 hard-boiled eggs
1 teaspoon sea salt
1 teaspoon chilli powder

Place the salt and chilli in a small bowl and mix together. Chop the hard-boiled eggs in half and then dip the flat side into the chilli mix.
Serve salt side up on a plate.

☞ Tip

Foods that are high in vitamin B improve the quality of your sleep. Legumes, eggs, salmon and meat are all high in vitamin B.

Curried Egg Dip

Prep time: 10 minutes
Serves: 2

Utensils:
Measuring spoons
Lemon Juicer
Mixing bowl
Serving bowl

2 hard-boiled eggs
1 teaspoon curry powder
1 teaspoon cumin powder
1 teaspoon lemon juice

Place the eggs in a mixing bowl and mash until smooth. Add all the remained ingredients and mix thoroughly.
Serve with a selection of fresh vegetable sticks.

100g (3½oz) tuna in spring water
2 tablespoons low fat natural plain yoghurt
4 tablespoons mixed herbs
1 small tomato, chopped into small cubes
Squeeze lemon or lime juice

In a mixing bowl place the tuna and yoghurt and mix thoroughly. Add all the remaining ingredients and combine well.
Serve with a selection of vegetable sticks

Healthy Tuna Dip

Prep time: 15 minutes
Serves: 6

Utensils:
Mixing bowl
Sharp knife
Lemon squeezer
Measuring spoons
Serving plate/bowl

 Tip

Take the time to stop and enjoy the food you are eating. This will assist in the digetsion of your meal, and you can savour each mouthful!

Cucumber, Mint and Yoghurt dip

Prep time: 15 minutes
Serves: 6

Utensils:
Mixing bowl
Sharp knives
Measuring spoons

1 Lebanese cucumber, chopped into small cubes
1 tablespoon chopped fresh mint
100g (3½oz) plain low fat yoghurt
1 teaspoon lemon juice

Place the all the ingredients in a mixing bowl and mix thoroughly.
Serve with a yummy selection of vegetable sticks.

100g (3½oz) hard tofu
1 teaspoon olive oil
1 teaspoon dried basil
1 teaspoon dried thyme
50g (1¾oz) cherry tomatoes

Combine the olive oil, basil and thyme in a mixing bowl. Place the tofu in the herb mixture and turn until all sides are coated.
Chop 4 skewers in half with a sharp knife.
Place a cube of tofu and then a cherry tomato and repeat once for each skewer. Place skewers on a plate to serve.

Marinated Tofu Cubes and Cherry Tomato Skewers

Serves: 8 skewers

Utensils:
Skewers
Sharp knife
Mixing bowl
Serving plate

Roasted Garlic, Broccoli and Cannellini Bean Dip

Prep time: 15 minutes
Cooking time: 20 minutes
Serves/Makes: 6

Utensils:
Blender
Roasting pans
Juicer
Mixing bowls
Spoons

6 slices soy and linseed or multigrain bread
2 cups of broccoli, roasted
4 whole garlic cloves, peeled
2 tablespoons extra virgin olive oil
2 teaspoons dried chilli or paprika
1 x 250g (8 fl oz) tin cannellini beans, rinsed and drained
¼ cup roasted almonds
2 tablespoons lemon juice
Parsley to garnish

Preheat oven to 140°C (275°F/Gas Mark 1). Cut the bread into 30–40mm (xx inch) rounds using a cookie cutter. Place on a tray and toast in oven for 5–10 minutes or until golden brown.

Increase the oven heat to 160°C (300F°/Gas Mark 2). Mix broccoli, garlic, olive oil and chilli together on a tray and place in the oven for approximately 15–20 minutes. Remove tray and cool mixture for 10 minutes.

Place broccoli mixture, drained and rinsed cannellini beans, almonds and lemon juice in a food processor and blend until smooth.

To serve, place approximately 1 teaspoon of the broccoli mixture on toasted bread rounds and sprinkle with a little parsley.

Spiced Hummus

1 cup chickpeas, soaked overnight
2 cups water for soaking
2–3 tablespoons tahini
2 cups water for boiling
3 garlic clover
2 tablespoons extra virgin olive oil
1 teaspoon fennel seeds, cumin seeds or any spices to add flavour
Pepper and sea salt to taste (but not too much salt)

Rinse soaked chickpeas with cold water, place in a saucepan and cover with water. Boil until soft approx 20 minutes. Set aside the boiling water in a jug or bowl and keep to add to mixture later. Place the chickpeas, garlic, tahini, olive oil and spices in a food processor and blend until soft but slightly nutty in texture. Add a little of the boiling water to make the mixture smoother. Spoon mixture into a bowl and season to taste. Cover and leave in the fridge and use when needed. Serve with freshly chopped vegetables.

Prep time: Soak chickpeas over night
Cooking time: 20 minutes
Serves/Makes: 6

Utensils:
Bowl for soaking
Saucepan
Food processor
Spoons
Serving ramekin or bowl

Steamed Fish Balls with Coriander and Chilli Dipping Sauce

Prep time: 20 minutes
Cooking time: 10 minutes
Makes: 20 pieces

Utensils:
Food processor
Grated
Mixing bowls
Sharp knives
Steamer
Spoons

Fish balls:
400g (14oz) fresh tuna
2–3 tablespoons tamari
1 tablespoon grated fresh ginger
1 garlic clove, crushed
½ cup chopped coriander (cilantro)
1 large grated carrot
1 cup grated sweet potato (yam)
Spelt or rice flour to coat patties

Dipping sauce:
¼ cup tamari
4 tablespoons finely chopped coriander (cilantro)
1 small fresh chilli, de-seeded and finely chopped
2 teaspoons honey

To make dipping sauce: Combine all ingredients in a small serving bowl. Set aside.

Place all the fish ball ingredients in a blender except the spelt flour. Blend ingredients well. Shape into 20 round balls and toss lightly in the spelt flour.

Place in a steamer for 8–10 minutes, turning them once.

Serve on a platter with dipping sauce in the middle.

Tomato and Yoghurt Dip

Prep time: 15 minutes
Serves: 6

Utensils:
Mixing bowl
Sharp knife
Measuring cup
Serving bowl

200g (7oz) low-fat natural plain yoghurt
2 ripe tomatoes, skinned and finely chopped
2 teaspoons extra virgin olive oil
1 tablespoon chopped fresh herbs (basil, mint, parsley or chives, or all!)

Put the yoghurt into a bowl and stir in the tomatoes, oil and herbs. Add seasoning to taste. Serve with freshly chopped vegetable sticks.

☞ Tip

Keep fresh, unsalted and raw nuts and seeds in your desk for a great vegetarian protein snack.

1 large carrot, finely grated
1 cup light cottage cheese
¼ cup chopped coriander (cilantro)
1 garlic glove, crushed
Juice of half a lemon
2 slices spelt bread or multigrain bread
1 tomato sliced
Sea salt to season

In a large bowl add the carrots and cottage cheese, stir lightly. Add the coriander, garlic and lemon juice to taste. Toast the spelt bead and spread with the cottage cheese dip. Place a sliced tomato on top and sprinkle with sea salt to taste.

Carrot, Coriander and Cottage Cheese dip

Prep time: 5–10 minutes
Serves: 2

Utensils:
Grater
Measuring cups
Garlic crusher
Large mixing bowl
Juicer

Stuffed Tofu Tomatoes (page 125)

Lunch

A healthy lunch will help set you up for the rest of the day. It will help you avoid the 3pm low when chocolate seems so appealing and will also keep you from blowing out at dinner time. Keeping lunch interesting and free from refined carbohydrates is the trick. The more processed your lunch, the quicker it will digest, leaving you wanting the 'bad foods' more!

Spice up your lunch with any of the following lunch recipes or use them as a small dinner. Enjoy!

Cauliflower and Almond Salad

50g (1¾oz) blanched whole almonds, cut into slivers
4 baby cauliflower (or ½ regular cauliflower, cut into large pieces)
8 button mushrooms, stalks removed and sliced thinly
2 inner stalks celery, cut into thin sticks
2 handfuls baby spinach leaves, washed, dried, excess stems removed

Dressing:
2 teaspoons almond oil (or walnut oil)
1½ tablespoons extra virgin olive oil
1–2 teaspoons verjuice
Salt, freshly ground pepper

Preheat oven to 180°C (350°F/Gas Mark 4) and toast the almonds until golden brown.
Bring a large saucepan of lightly salted water to the boil. Drop in cauliflower for 2 minutes. Drain then refresh by soaking in icy cold water for 20 minutes. Drain very well and pat dry in a clean cloth.
Mix the dressing ingredients together.
In a large bowl, toss all the salad ingredients with the dressing. Season to taste and allow to sit for at least 20 minutes before serving.

Prep time: 15 minutes
Cooking time: 5 minutes
Serves: 4–6

Utensils:
Saucepan
Ice bowl
Serving bowls

Barbecued Lamb Skewers with Yoghurt Dipping Sauce

Prep time: 15 minutes
Cooking time: 6–10 minutes
Serves: 4

Utensils:
2 mixing bowls
Lemon juicer
Measuring spoons
Serving plates

Lamb:
800g (1¾lb) lamb fillets, cut into cubes
Juice of 1 lemon
2 tablespoons olive oil
1–2 teaspoons of salt

Dipping sauce:
200g (7oz) low fat yoghurt
2 teaspoons of sumac
1 teaspoon chilli powder
1 teaspoon dried mint
1 garlic clove, crushed
1 teaspoon salt

In a mixing bowl stir together the lamb ingredients and leave to marinate for 30–60 minutes.
In another bowl mix together all the dipping sauce ingredients and cover with plastic until ready to use.
Preheat the barbecue. Thread the lamb onto the skewers; 6–8 pieces per skewer. Cook on the barbecue for 3–5 minutes each side.
Serve with the dipping sauce and a green salad.

Barley and Mushroom Risotto

Prep time: 10 minutes
Cooking time: 30 minutes
Serves: 2

Utensils:
Food processor
Measuring spoons
Mixing bowl
Measuring cups
Small bowls for the
ingredients
Saucepan

150g (5oz) pearled barley (soaked for one hour)
¼ cup peeled carrot
¼ cup celery, hearts if possible
½ cup mushrooms (flat, button or brown)
1 clove garlic
1 onion, coarsely chopped
2 tablespoons olive oil
1 litre (2 pints) hot chicken or vegetable stock or miso soup
2 tablespoons parsley

Place carrot, celery, mushrooms, garlic and onion in a blender and process until coarsely chopped.

In a saucepan, heat olive oil then sauté the processed mixture until soft; approximately 3–4 minutes. Add the drained barley and stir through.

Add 3–4 ladles of hot stock and simmer until barley is tender. Add more stock if needed.

When cooked, add parsley and season to taste.

Serve with any protein and a salad.

☞ Tip

Selenium is very high in antioxidents and can easily be found in nuts. But if you're not a fan of nuts, increase your consumption of full-grained bread, tuna, barley, mushroom, garlic, chicken and tomatoes

Beef and Vegetable Soup

1kg (2lb) lean ground beef
½ teaspoons garlic
1 tablespoon olive oil
1 large onion, chopped finely.
¼ teaspoon cumin powder
¼ teaspoon pepper
Juice of half a lemon
½ lemon, zested
½ cup chopped celery
1 x 400g (14oz) tin kidney beans, drained
½ cabbage, chopped
1 cup red capsicum, roughly chopped
2 large carrots, chopped
1 x 400g (14 oz) can tomatoes chopped
1 litre (2 pints) vegetable or beef stock
Chopped parsley for garnish

In a large saucepan place the olive oil, onion and garlic and cook until golden brown. Once cooked add the lean group beef, cumin and pepper and cook until brown. Add all remaining ingredients except parsley to the large saucepan and bring to boil. Reduce heat and simmer, covered, for 1 hour. Ladle into bowls and garnish with parsley to serve.

Preparation time: 15 minutes
Cooking time: 1 hour
Serving: 6–8 people

Utensils:
Sharp knife
Large saucepan
Measuring cups
Measuring spoons
Lemon zester and juicer
Serving bowls

Cashew Fritters with Salsa Topping

Prep time: 10–15 minutes
Cooking time: 10 minutes
Makes 6 fritters

Utensils:
Mixing bowl
Frying pan
Measuring cups
Serving plate
Sharp knives

Cashew fritters:
½ large onion, finely chopped
1 tablespoon olive oil
1 cup raw cashews, finely ground
½ bunch fresh basil, finely chopped (or 2 dessertspoons dried basil)
1 egg, lightly beaten
1 dessertspoon tamari (or 2 pinches salt)

Salsa topping:
1 tomato, diced
2 cloves garlic, diced or crushed
1 dessertspoon tamari (or 2 pinches salt)
2 teaspoons tomato paste

To garnish:
20g (¾oz) feta or goat's cheese
Fresh basil or coriander (cilantro)

To make fritters: Cook onion in heated olive oil until soft. Combine the onion, cashews, basil, egg and tamari in a bowl. Stir until thick and sticky.
Use a dessertspoon to form fritters and cook in a lightly oiled frying pan on medium for 5 minutes each side.

To make salsa: Sauté tomato and garlic in a pan for about 10 minutes or until pureed. Add tomato paste and tamari and stir.

Serve fritters on a plate with salsa on top. Place slithers of feta or goat's cheese on top of salsa and garnish with fresh basil leaves or coriander.

400g (14oz) lean chicken mince (ground chicken)
or tuna
1–2 tablespoons tamari
1 tablespoon grated fresh ginger
1 garlic clove crushed
½ cup chopped coriander (cilantro)
1 large carrot, grated
1 cup grated sweet potato (yam)
Spelt or wholemeal flour to coat patties
Olive oil for the pan

Place all the ingredients, except the spelt flour, in a food processor and blend until smooth. Transfer the blended ingredients into a bowl. Shape into four or six burgers and toss lightly in the spelt flour. Heat a little olive oil and cook patties for 3–5 minutes each side. Alternatively brush patties with olive oil and bake in the oven for 10 minutes turning once.
Serve the chicken patties with steamed vegetables.

Chicken and Vegetable Patties

Preparation time: 15 minutes
Cooking time: 6–10 minutes
or oven cooking time 20 minutes
Makes 4–6 patties

Utensils:
Food processor
Frying pan
Zester
Serving plates

Chicken Breast with Raw Tomato and Red Capsicum Sauce

2 x 200g (7oz) chicken breast
Salt and pepper
1 teaspoon dried oregano
1 teaspoon olive oil

Raw sauce:

150g (5oz) ripe fresh tomatoes, skinned and quartered
1 large red capsicum, or 1 small red and 1 small yellow capsicum, cored, de-seeded and quartered
1 tablespoon fresh parsley
1 tablespoon freshly grated parmesan cheese
1 tablespoon olive oil

Preheat oven to 180°C (350°F/Gas Mark 4). In a bowl mix the chicken breast, salt and pepper, oregano and olive oil. Place the chicken on a baking tray and cover the tray with foil. Cook in the oven for approximately 15–20 minutes.
Put the tomato quarters in a food processor with the capsicum, parsley, grated parmesan cheese and 1 tablespoon olive oil and process to a thick sauce. Place the cooked chicken breast on a plate and cover with the raw tomato sauce. Serve at once with a salad or vegetables.
Freeze any leftover sauce.

Preparation time: 10 minutes
Cooking time: 20 hour
Serves: 2

Utensils:
Foil
Baking tray
Food processor
Grater
Sharp knife
Serving plate

Chilli Turkey

Prep time: 10 minutes
Cooking time: 35 minutes
Serves: 4

Utensils:
Large frying pan
Sharp knife
Serving plates

2 onions, finely chopped
2 garlic cloves, crushed
2 tablespoons olive oil
500g (1lb) turkey mince (ground turkey)
2 teaspoons of chilli powder
1 tablespoon Tabasco sauce
1 teaspoon cumin
1 teaspoon pepper
200g (7oz) tinned organic navy beans, drained and washed
200g (7oz) tinned organic kidney beans
½ cup water
½ teaspoon sea salt
½ cup chopped fresh coriander (cilantro)
1 red capsicum, diced
400g (14oz) tin crushed tomatoes

In a large frying pan, sauté the onion and garlic in olive oil. Add the turkey and stir over medium heat for 10–15 minutes. Add the chilli, Tabasco, cumin and pepper and cook for a further 5 minutes.

Add the navy beans, water and sea salt and cook for a further 15 minutes. Add the coriander, capsicum and tomatoes and cook for a further 10–15 minutes. Serve over steamed vegetables or with a salad.

Clear Prawn Thai Soup

8 Chinese or button mushrooms, fresh or dried,
cut into quarters
4 cups chicken or vegetable stock
2 cloves garlic, crushed
1 tablespoon grated ginger
1½ tablespoons rice wine vinegar
2 teaspoons of honey
12 green prawns, shelled
4 spring onions sliced
2 stalks lemongrass, halved lengthways and gently
crushed to release the flavour
1 red Thai chilli
Salt and pepper to season
Fresh coriander (cilantro) to garnish

Prep time: 35 minutes
Cooking time: 20–30
minutes
Serves: 2

Utensils:
Heavy-based pan
Sharp knives
Serving bowls

To rehydrate dried mushrooms, place them in
a bowl, cover with boiling water and soak for
approximately 35 minutes. Place the stock, garlic,
ginger, rice wine vinegar and honey in a heavy-
based pan. Bring to a gentle simmer, stirring
constantly.
Add the prawns, spring onions, lemongrass,
chilli and mushrooms and continue to simmer for
20 minutes. Taste and adjust the seasoning to your
own liking. Remove the lemongrass and serve the
soup garnished with freshly chopped coriander.

Curried Sweet Potato Soup

Prep time: 15 minutes
Cooking time: 30 minutes
Serves: 6

Utensils:
Food processor (optional)
Measuring spoons
Mixing bowl
Measuring cups
Small bowls for the ingredients
Saucepan

1kg (2lb) orange-fleshed sweet potato (yam)
1.5 litres (2 pints) boiling water
4 tablespoons of miso paste
Sea salt and pepper
1 cup lentils, pre-soaked for 1 hour
¼ cup celery, chopped finely
4 tomatoes, chopped finely
2 carrots, chopped finely
1 red pepper, de-seeded and chopped finely
¼ cup barley, washed and drained
400g (14oz) fresh white beans (soaked overnight) or organic tinned beans
1 teaspoon fresh chilli
1–2 garlic cloves
1 teaspoon fresh ginger
1 teaspoon cumin powder
1 teaspoon coriander (cilantro) powder
½ cup parsley or coriander (cilantro) leaves

Peel the sweet potato and cut into small cubes. Place in a heavy-based saucepan with the boiling water, miso paste, sea salt and pepper and bring to the boil. Add lentils, barely, celery, carrots, red peppers and tomatoes. Simmer for 15 minutes or until vegetables are soft.

Drain the beans and rinse. Add the beans, chilli, garlic, ginger, and cumin and coriander powder to the saucepan and stir well.

You can process the soup in a blender or food processor at this stage if you want a smoother version.

If the soup is too thick for your liking, add extra boiling water. Taste for salt, pepper then scatter with parsley or coriander.

1 large onion, finely chopped
2 garlic cloves
1 tablespoon olive oil
400g (14oz) chicken breast, chopped into strips
4 tablespoons good quality curry powder
2 x 200g (7oz) tin crushed tomatoes
2 cups water or vegetable or chicken stock
6 cups mixed vegetables, roughly chopped
(carrots, capsicum, carrots, cauliflower and peas)
½ cup chopped fresh coriander (cilantro)

Sauté the onions and garlic in olive oil until brown in a large saucepan. Add the chicken strips and curry powder and cook for 5–10 minutes. Add the tinned tomatoes, water or stock and all the vegetables and cook for approximately 15 minutes over medium heat,
Once the curry is cooked stir through the coriander and serve with rice, Quinoa or over steamed vegetable.

Easy Vegetable and Chicken Curry

Prep time: 15 minutes
Cooking time: 25 minutes
Serves: 2–4

Utensils:
Large saucepan
Sharp knife
Chopping board
Serving bowls

Fish Vindaloo

Prep time: 30–40 minutes
Cooking time: 10 minutes
Serves: 4

Utensils:
Heavy-based frying pan
Sharp knife
Measuring spoons
Serving plates

1 tablespoon extra virgin olive oil
4 cloves garlic
3 teaspoon fresh ginger, grated
1 teaspoon cinnamon
2 teaspoons ground cardamom
1 teaspoon fenugreek seed
1 teaspoon hot chilli powder
½ teaspoons sweet paprika
1 teaspoon ground turmeric
1 teaspoon mustard powder
500g (1lb) firm white-flesh fish, cut into 3cm (1in) cubes
1 tablespoon apple cider vinegar or balsamic vinegar
1–2 cups homemade vegetable stock

Drizzle oil into a heavy-based frying pan. Cook garlic and ginger over a low heat for 1 minute. Add spices and cook for a further 2–3 minutes until fragrant.
Add fish and gently toss to coat with spices.
Pour in the vinegar and stock. Cover and cook over a low heat for 15–20 minutes.
Serve with streamed vegetables.

Guilt-free Mashed Potatoes

Prep time: 10–15 minutes
Cooking time: 20 minutes
Serves: 4–6 people

Utensils:
Large saucepan
Food processor
Serving bowl

2–3 large potatoes, scrubbed and cut into 3cm (1in) chunks
1½ cups cauliflower florets
2 tablespoons olive oil
½ avocado
1 teaspoon cumin
Salt and pepper to taste
Parsley for serving
A little hot water if needed to moisten

Place the chunks of potato in a large saucepan of water and bring to the boil. When the water is boiling add the cauliflower and cook for 20 minutes or until soft.

Place all remaining ingredients into a food processor with the potato and cauliflower and blend until soft and fluffy.

Serve the mash with a little olive oil, sea salt and parsley sprinkled on top.

☞ Tip

Cauliflower is a fantastic cancer fighter, helping to prevent lung, stomach, breast and bladder cancer. Simply by lightly steaming cauliflower you will release more of the cancer-fighting nutrients such as beta-carotene.

Lamb and Bean Soup

2 onions, chopped
2 tablespoons olive oil
500g (1lb) diced lamb
¾ teaspoon ground cinnamon
½ teaspoons smoked paprika
½ teaspoons ground ginger
½ teaspoon pepper
3 celery sticks, chopped
2 carrots, diced
400g (14oz) tinned organic chickpeas, drained
and washed
½ cup red lentils (soaked for 6–8 hours)
1.5 litres (3 pints) vegetable, chicken or beef stock
½ teaspoons sea salt
½ cup parsley
400g (14oz) tin crushed tomatoes

Prep time: 10 minutes
Cooking time: 35 minutes
Serves: 4

Utensils:
Large saucepan
Sharp knife
Serving bowls

Sauté the onions in olive oil. Add the lamb and stir over medium heat for 10–15 minutes. Add the cinnamon, paprika, ginger and pepper, cook for a further 5 minutes.
Add the celery, carrots, chickpeas, lentils, stock and sea salt. Reduce the heat and simmer for an hour. Add the parsley and tomatoes and cook for a further 15 minutes. Serve in hot bowls with a wedge of lemon.

Lentil and Spinach Soup

Preparation time: 15 minutes
Cooking time: 1 hour
Serving: 6–8 people

Utensils:
Large saucepan
Zester
Sharp knife
Serving bowls

250g (8oz) small brown or green lentils
2 garlic cloves, smashed
2 bay leaves
2 tablespoons olive oil
1 onion, finely chopped
2 leeks, chopped
2 carrots, peeled and diced
2 celery stalks, finely sliced
400g tinned of crushed organic tomatoes
400g (14oz) can chickpeas, drained
500g (1lb) spinach, roughly chopped
Sea salt and pepper
2 tablespoons parsley, roughly a lemon
¼ lemon, juice and zest

Rinse the lentils and place in a pot with the garlic cloves, bay leaves and 1.5 litres (3 pints) of cold water. Cook for 30 minutes or until almost tender, skimming occasionally.

Meanwhile, heat the olive oil in a large saucepan. Add the onion, leek, carrot and celery and cook, stirring well, for 10 minutes. Add the tomatoes, stir well, and then add the lentils and their water.

Simmer for 20 minutes until nice and soupy. Add the chickpeas, spinach, salt and pepper and simmer for a further 10 minutes or longer, adding extra water if necessary. Stir in the parsley, lemon zest and juice and serve in warmed soup bowls.

50g (1¾oz) whole almonds, roughly crushed
4 baby cauliflower (or ½ regular cauliflower, cut into large pieces)
200g (7oz) tin mackerel
8 button mushrooms, stalks removed and thinly sliced
2 inner stalks celery, cut into thin sticks
2 handfuls baby spinach leaves, washed, dried, excess stems removed

Dressing:
2 teaspoons almond oil (or walnut oil)
1½ tablespoons extra virgin olive oil
1–2 teaspoons verjuice
Salt and freshly ground pepper

Preheat the oven to 180°C (350°F/Gas Mark 4) and toast the almonds until golden brown; approximately 5–6 minutes.
Bring a large saucepan of lightly salted water to the boil. Drop in cauliflower for 2 minutes. Drain and refresh by soaking in icy cold water for 20 minutes. Drain very well and pat dry with a clean cloth.
Mix the dressing ingredients together.
In a large bowl, toss the mackerel and all the salad ingredients with the dressing. Taste for seasoning and allow to sit for at least 20 minutes before serving.

Mackerel, Cauliflower and Almond Salad

Prep time: 15 minutes
Cooking time: 5 minutes
Serves: 1

Utensils:
Saucepan
Ice bowl
Serving bowls

Moroccan Marinated Chickpeas

Prep time: 20 minutes
Serves: 4

Utensils:
Zester
2 mixing bowls
Sharp knives
Whisk
Serving plate

400g (14oz) tin organic chickpeas
1 large carrot, grated
10 cherry tomatoes, halved
2 tablespoons organic currants
1 cup finely chopped parsley
½ cup finely chopped fresh mint
2 cups wild rocket

Chickpea dressing:
½ orange, juiced
1 teaspoon orange zest
½ lemon, juiced
1 teaspoon lemon zest
½ lime, juiced
1 teaspoon lime zest
2 tablespoons extra virgin olive oil
1 teaspoon organic honey

To make dressing, whisk together all ingredients in a small bowl.

Add all remaining ingredients into a bowl and mix thoroughly.

Pour the dressing over the chickpea mixture. Combine thoroughly and then leave for 30 minutes so the dressing can permeate the chickpeas.

Serve the chickpeas on a bed of rocket.

Mushroom and Prawn Risotto with Barley

Prep time: 10 minutes
Cooking time: 30 minutes
Serves: 2

Utensils:
Food processor
Measuring spoons
Mixing bowl
Measuring cups
Small bowls for the ingredients
Saucepan

150g (5oz) of pearled barley
¼ cup peeled carrot, roughly chopped
¼ cup celery, hearts if possible
½ cup mushrooms, flat, button and/or brown
1 clove garlic
1 onion
2 tablespoons olive oil
200g (7oz) of green prawns, shelled
1 litre (2 pints) chicken or vegetable stock or miso soup
2 tablespoons parsley
Salt and pepper

Soak pearl barley in warm water for 30 minutes.

In a food processor place carrot, celery, mushrooms, garlic and onion and blend until coarsely chopped.

Heat the olive oil in a saucepan and sauté the mixture, with the prawns, until soft; approximately 5 minutes.

Add the drained barley and stir thoroughly.

Add 3–4 ladles of hot stock and simmer until barley is tender. Add more stock if needed. When cooked, add parsley and season to taste.

Serve with any protein and a salad.

Rich Roasted Tomato and Vegetable Sauce

6 tomatoes, halved
4 zucchinis cut into 1cm (½in) rounds
1 Spanish (red) onion, cut into 1cm rounds
4 medium carrots cut in 1cm rounds
1 cup rocket
4 cloves of garlic, skins removed
2 tablespoons basil
2 tablespoons marjoram
1 tablespoon cumin powder
¼ cup water
4 tablespoons olive oil
Sea salt and pepper

Preheat oven to 160°C (300°F/Gas Mark 2).
Place all the chopped vegetables, herbs, cumin
and water into a baking tray and cook in the oven
for 30–40 minutes until brown and caramelised.
Stir every 10–15 minutes to prevent burning. Once
cooked, leave to cool for 15 minutes.
Place vegetables into a food processor with the
olive oil, salt and pepper and blend until smooth.
Serve with wholemeal pasta, mashed potatoes
or crusty bread.

Prep time: 15minute
Cooking time: 40 minutes
Serves: 4

Utensils:
Chopping board
Sharp knife
Baking tray
Food processor
Serving bowl

Italian Roast Vegetables with Quinoa

Prep time: 5 minutes
Cooking time: 15 minutes
Serves: 2

Utensils:
Roasted pan
Saucepan
Sharp knives
Serving plate

1 red pepper, chopped into 1cm (½in) rounds
1 green pepper, chopped into 1cm (½in) rounds
2 red onions, chopped into 1cm (½in) rounds
2 zucchinis, sliced into 1cm (½in) rounds
1 large field mushroom, chopped into 1cm (½in) slices
1 punnet of cherry tomatoes
6 garlic cloves, skins removed
3 tablespoon extra virgin olive oil
3 tablespoons fresh thyme (basil or parsley also work well)
¼ cup water
Sea salt and pepper
1 cup quinoa
2 cups of water, for cooking the quinoa

Wash and slice all the vegetables, leaving the tomatoes and garlic whole.

Toss all the vegetables and garlic together in a large roasting pan with the olive oil, thyme, ¼ cup water, salt and pepper. Place in a preheated oven at 180°C (350°F/Gas Mark 4) for 15–20 minutes or until the vegetables are soft and have turned golden brown.

Meanwhile, rinse the quinoa very well (otherwise it can taste bitter). Place in a saucepan with the 2 cups of water. Bring to the boil then cover and simmer until cooked. This should take about 15 minutes.

Serve the quinoa with the roasted vegetables on top. You can also add goat's or feta cheese over the vegetables before serving.

Raw Salad with Tuna, Sweet Agave and Avocado Dressing

Prep time: 23–35 minutes
Cooking time: 6–8 minutes
Serves: 4

Utensils:
Blender
Lemon zester
Lemon juicer
Measuring spoons
Mixing bowl
Measuring cups
Small bowls for the ingredients

Avocado and agave dressing:

1 tablespoon agave nectar or honey
1 avocado, diced
2–3 red chillies, de-seeded and roughly chopped
(choose the small for a fiery taste or the large ones for a milder taste)
2 tablespoons apple cider vinegar
2 cloves garlic, crushed
1 tablespoon mixed zest, (orange, lemon and lime)
$1/3$ cup fresh mint leaves
$1/3$ cup fresh basil leaves
$1/4$ cup olive oil
2 tablespoons water

Salad:

400g (14oz) tin tuna in spring water (optional)
1 red capsicum, trimmed and cut into 2–3cm (1in) lengths
1 cup green beans, trimmed and cut into 2–3cm (1in) lengths
1 cup raw broccoli, trimmed and cut into florets
1 cup grated beetroot
1 cup grated carrot
2 cups fresh wild or baby rocket, washed

Combine all dressing ingredients in a food processor or jug blender and blend until smooth. Set aside until needed. In a large mixing bowl, toss briefly to combine the tuna, capsicum, beans, broccoli, beetroot and carrot. Pour the dressing over the top or stir dressing through salad before serving. Place a handful of the rocket on each plate and top with the vegetable salad.

115

Salmon with Roasted Beetroot and Apple Salad

Prep time: 10 minutes
Cooking time: 20 minutes
Serves: 3–4

Utensils:
Roasting pan
Baking tray
Mixing bowl
Serving plate

3 medium beetroots, peeled and cut in quarters
2 x 200g (7oz) salmon fillet, seasoned with olive oil, salt and pepper
3 medium green apples, cored and sliced into half moons
½ cup watercress
½ cup rocket

Dressing:
1 tablespoon horseradish
1 tablespoon raspberry vinegar
3 tablespoon of extra virgin olive oil
½ teaspoon brown sugar
3 tablespoons low fat natural yogurt

Preheat oven to 180°C (350°F/Gas Mark 4). Place beetroot on a tray and drizzle over a little olive oil then season with salt and pepper. Bake in oven for 20 minutes. Remove from the oven and leave to sit until room temperature.

Cove the salmon in foil and place on a baking tray. Cook in the oven for approximately 15 minutes.

Remove salmon from foil and flake in a bowl with a fork. Mix in the roasted beetroot, apple and watercress.

Place the rocket on a serving plate with the beetroot and salmon mix on top.

To make the dressing, mix all the ingredients together and then pour over the salad to serve.

2 ripe avocados, chopped
Juice of 1 lemon
1 garlic glove, chopped
1 tablespoon olive oil
1 tablespoon full-fat natural plain yoghurt
1 teaspoon honey
2 cups spiral spelt pasta
Parsley for garnish

Place all ingredients except pasta in a food processor and pulse until a creamy consistency.
Cook the spelt pasta until slightly softer than al dente. Drain and place in a serving bowl and mix through a little olive oil.
Stir the avocado sauce through the pasta and serve with a little parsley on top.

Spelt Pasta with Creamy Avocado Sauce

Prep time: 5–10 minutes
Serves: 2

Utensils:
Food processor
Spoons
Mixing bowl
Juicer
Serving bowl

 Tip

Reduce your alcohol intake to 2 glasses of wine or 2 beers a day, with 3 alcohol-free days a week.

Spicy Tomato and Chickpea Stew

Prep time: 10 minutes
Cooking time: 20–25
minutes
Serves: 4

Utensils:
Saucepan
Drainer
Mixing bowl
Measuring spoons
Sharp knives

Stew:
1 tablespoon olive oil
2 onions, sliced
200g (7oz) fresh capsicum, chopped
4 cloves garlic, crushed
1 tablespoon ground cumin
1 tablespoon ground coriander (cilantro)
1 teaspoon sweet paprika
2 x 400g (14oz) tins chopped organic tomatoes
1 tablespoon organic honey
425g (15oz) organic tomato puree
2 x 425g (15oz) tins organic chickpeas, drained
and rinsed
1 cup chopped flat leaf parsley
Salt and freshly ground pepper

Heat the olive oil in a frying pan, stir in the onions
and cook for 4 minutes over moderate heat. Add
the chopped capsicum and stir for 4–5 minutes.

Mix in the garlic and spices and cook for 1–2
minutes. Stir in the chopped tomatoes, honey,
tomato puree and chickpeas.

Bring to the boil, then reduce the heat and
simmer for about 15 minutes.

Season well with salt and freshly ground pepper,
stir in the parsley and serve with a salad.

6 free range eggs, whisked in a bowl with
seasoning and chopped chives
1 bunch of asparagus, lightly blanched
200g (7oz) green beans, lightly blanched
½ medium Spanish (red) onion, finely sliced
8 sundried tomatoes, finely sliced
1 teaspoon chopped chives
1 teaspoon sesame seeds
Sea salt and pepper to taste

Lightly spray a frying pan with olive oil spray and
heat gently. Place a third of the egg mixture into
the frying pan and cook until mixture sets.
Turn omelette out and repeat until all mixture has
been used.
Roll omelettes into a cylinder shape and then
slice into circles, approximately 1cm (½in) wide.
Combine all ingredients except for omelette and
sesame seeds in a bowl and gently mix together.
Arrange salad on a serving platter with omelette
circles and sprinkle with sesame seeds. This is
best served at room temperature.

Sundried Tomato, Egg Omelette and Asparagus Salad

Prep time: 20 minutes
Cooking time: 10 minutes
Serves: 2–4

Utensils:
Large frying pan
Large saucepan for blanching
Sharp knife
Whisk
Serving bowl

Spring Bouillabaisse

Prep time: 15 minutes
Cooking time: 20 minutes
Serves: 4–6

Utensils:
Large saucepan
Sharp knives
Zester
Serving bowls

2 tablespoons extra virgin olive oil
2 onions, thinly sliced
2 leeks, sliced
1 cup finely chopped fennel
2 x 400g (14oz) tins chopped organic tomatoes
4 cloves garlic, minced
1 sprig fresh thyme
1 bay leaf
Zest of 1 large orange
Salt and pepper
200g (7oz) scallops
500g (1lb) fresh prawns, peeled and de-veined
500g (1lb) salmon, cut into 2cm (1in) cubes
9 cups water
1 pinch saffron threads

Heat the olive oil in a large saucepan, and add the onions, leeks, fennel, chopped tomatoes and garlic. Cook and stir over a low heat for a few minutes until all the vegetables are soft. Stir in the thyme, bay leaf and orange zest.

Pour the boiling water into the saucepan then add the scallops and prawns and stir. Season to taste with salt and black pepper. Turn up the heat to high and boil for about 3 minutes to allow the oil and water to combine.

Add the fish and reduce the heat to medium. Continue cooking for 12 to 15 minutes or until fish is cooked. The fish should be opaque and tender, but still firm. Fish should not be falling apart. Taste the bouillabaisse and adjust the seasoning. Stir in saffron, then pour soup into warmed soup bowls. Serve immediately.

Wild Mushroom Soup

Prep time: 10 minutes
Cooking time: 30 minutes
Serves: 2

Utensils:
Large saucepan
Sharp knife
Whisk
Garlic crusher

1½ teaspoons olive oil
1 onion, finely chopped
500g (1lb) wild mushrooms, wiped clean
500g (1lb) cultivated mushrooms (button or brown mushrooms are fine)
2 garlic cloves, crushed
Few sprigs thyme
2 tomatoes, chopped
2 tablespoons tomato paste
1.2 litres (2¼ pints) vegetable stock or miso
2 tablespoons low fat yoghurt
Pinch sea or vegetable salt and pepper
2 tablespoons flat leaf parsley, chopped

Heat the oil in a frying pan and cook the onion for 10 minutes or until it starts to soften, without colouring.

Wipe the mushrooms with a damp cloth, trim the stalks and slice finely.

Add the mushrooms, garlic and thyme to the pan and cook for 5 minutes. Add the tomato paste and tomatoes and the stock and simmer gently for 20 minutes or until tender.

Whisk in yoghurt (it may curdle but it will taste exactly the same), sea salt and pepper to taste.

Sprinkle with parsley and serve in warm soup bowls.

Stuffed Tofu Tomatoes

6 firm ripe large tomatoes
5 stalks spinach, roughly chopped
¼ cup fresh basil
1 tablespoon pine nuts, raw
1 cup hard tofu, crumbled
2 teaspoons olive oil
1 small clove garlic, crushed
Sea salt and freshly ground pepper
1–2 tablespoons freshly grated sheep's feta cheese

Prep time: 15 minutes
Cooking time: 20 minutes
Serves: 6

Utensils:
Food processor
Sharp knifes
Mixing bowl
Saucepan

Cut the tops off the tomatoes, scoop out flesh and discard, then turn tomatoes upside down to drain. Wash the spinach, remove the stalks and tear leaves into large pieces and then place in saucepan. Cook over medium heat while stirring until soft; approximately 5 minutes.
Place the spinach and basil in a food processor and blend. Add pine nuts and process for a further 10 seconds.
Place spinach mix in a bowl. Add the tofu, olive oil, crushed garlic, salt and pepper and mix well. Fold in the grated feta cheese.
Place the tomatoes in a greased ovenproof dish. Spoon tofu mixture into the tomatoes and then bake in moderate oven for 15 to 20 minutes on 180°C (350°F/Gas Mark 4).
Serve warm with a green salad.

Tandoori Turkey Breasts

Prep time: 10 minutes
Cooking time: 10–20 minutes
Serves: 4

Utensils:
Mixing bowl
Lemon juicer
Garlic crusher
Measuring spoons
Serving plates

4 x 200g–250g (7oz–8oz) turkey breasts
200g (7oz) low-fat yoghurt
2 tablespoons tandoori powder
1 garlic clove, crushed
¼ cup chopped coriander (cilantro)
Olive oil for cooking

Place all the ingredients into a mixing bowl and combine thoroughly. Leave to sit for 20 minutes.

Heat the olive oil in a frying pan until medium to hot. Place the turkey in the frying pan and cook for approximately 10 minutes each side.

Serve the turkey breasts with steamed vegetables tossed with lemon juice and mint.

☞ Tip

Take a good quality multi-vitamin. This will ensure you are getting all of your recommended daily allowance (RDA).

Thai Fish and Squash Curry

Prep time: 30–40 minutes
Cooking time: 10 minutes
Serves: 4

Utensils:
Wok or large frying pan
Sharp knife
Measuring cups
Measuring spoons
Zester
Serving bowls

1 tbsp of olive oil
1 large Spanish (red) onion, sliced into thin wedges
½ red capsicum, thinly sliced
1 garlic clove, crushed
2 teaspoons red curry paste
½ teaspoon brown sugar
1 tablespoon fish sauce
500g (1lb) firm fish fillets, cut into pieces
500g (1lb) golden squash
100g (3½oz) sheep's yoghurt
2 cups water or fish stock
1 cup shredded basil leaves
1 cup coriander (cilantro) leaves
Juice of 1 lime
2 teaspoons lime zest

Heat oil in wok or large frying pan. Add onion, capsicum and garlic and cook for 1–2 minutes.

Stir in red curry paste and sugar and cook for 1 minute, until fragrant.

Add fish sauce and cook through for a minute. Add fish, squash, yoghurt and water or fish stock and cook for about 5–10 minutes or until cooked, stirring occasionally. Remove from heat, add the herbs, lime juice and zest and stir through gently.

Serve with steamed vegetables.

Toasted Quinoa Salad

¾ cup uncooked quinoa
Water for cooking quinoa
1 cup diced carrot
½ cup chopped red pepper
¼ cup minced parsley or coriander (cilantro)
2 sliced spring (green) onions
juice of 1 lemon and 1 lime (1–2 tablespoons of each)
1–1½ tablespoons tamari
2 cloves minced or pressed garlic
1 teaspoon Tabasco (chilli) sauce (or use a pinch of cayenne or a few red pepper flakes)

Rinse quinoa and drain. Put in a pot and dry toast until a few grains begin to pop. Add 1–1½ cups of water, bring to the boil, cover and simmer for about 15 minutes, or until the water is absorbed. Remove from heat and let stand for 10 minutes. Fluff with a fork and let cool. Mix carrot, red pepper, parsley and green onion in large bowl. Add cold quinoa and toss to combine. Whisk together lemon and lime juice, tamari, garlic and chilli sauce. Pour over the salad and combine well. Chill until serving time. You can also add a few fresh raw peas, fresh raw corn or fresh sliced raw greens to this recipe.

Prep time: 15 minutes
Cooking time: 30 minutes

Utensils:
Sharp knives
Large frying pan
Mixing bowl
Serving plates

Tofu Patties with Salad

Utensils:
Food processor
Sharp knife
Frying pan
Grater
Mixing bowl
Serving plate

1 small onion, finely chopped
2 large garlic cloves, crushed
1 tablespoon olive oil
200g (7oz) hard tofu, crumbled and drained of any excess liquid
2 tablespoons fresh red chilli, de-seeded and finely chopped
1 tablespoon soy sauce
1 tablespoon Worcestershire sauce
1 teaspoon cumin powder
1 teaspoon coriander (cilantro) powder
1 egg, lightly beaten
1 carrot, finely grated

Sauté the onion and garlic in olive oil in a saucepan until onion is slightly brown.

Place the tofu in a large bowl and mash with a fork, then stir in the onion-garlic mixture. Add the chilli, soy sauce, Worcestershire sauce, cumin, coriander, egg and carrot and mix well.

Place in a food processor and pulse to form a uniform texture. Add salt and pepper to taste. Refrigerate for 30 minutes.

With wet hands, shape tofu mixture into 8 to 10 patties and then place on a hot, lightly oiled frying pan. Handle the patties gently as they're delicate. Cook for 3–4 minutes on each side or until nicely browned.

These patties are especially tasty when served with a spicy sauce made of low-sodium soy sauce mixed with chilli sauce or barbecue sauce, topped with sautéed mushrooms and served with a green salad.

Tuna, Kidney Beans and Quinoa Salad with Harissa Dressing

Harissa dressing:
¼ cup olive oil
2 tablespoons lemon juice
2 teaspoons harissa or chilli
1 small clove garlic, crushed

Bean salad:
200g (7oz) tin of tuna in spring water
¼ cup cooked quinoa (optional)
100g (3½oz) tin organic kidney beans, drained and rinsed
½ cup celery, roughly chopped
1 cup baby spinach leaves
4 spring onions, finely chopped
12 cherry tomatoes, halved
$1/3$ cup chopped fresh mint
$1/3$ cup chopped fresh coriander (cilantro)

Place all the harissa dressing ingredients in a large jar and shake well to combine.
Combine the kidney beans, quinoa, spring onions, tomatoes, mint and coriander in a serving bowl and mix thoroughly.
Add the dressing and toss using two folks until all the ingredients are well coated.
Serve immediately.

Prep time: 5 minutes
Cooking time: 10–15 minutes
Serves: 2

Utensils:
Measuring spoons
Sharp knifes
2–3 mixing bowls
Juicer
Garlic crusher

Tuna and Zucchini Frittata

4 tablespoons olive oil
1 large onion, coarsely chopped
1 teaspoon chopped fresh thyme
1kg (2lb) zucchini grated, excess water squeezed out
6 large whole eggs
1 x 250g (8oz) tin tuna in spring water, drained
½ teaspoon crushed dried thyme (optional)
2 tablespoons chopped Italian parsley or fresh basil
½ teaspoon sea salt
½ teaspoon pepper

Preheat oven to 160°C (300F°/Gas Mark 2).
In a small frying pan over a medium heat sauté the olive oil, onions and thyme until brown. Add the zucchini to the onion mixture, cover and cook over medium heat, stirring occasionally, for 10–12 minutes. Leave to cool. Once cool, drain off any excess water if necessary.
In a bowl, beat the eggs lightly with a fork and then add the tuna, thyme and parsley or basil. Beat in the salt and pepper. Add the drained and cooled zucchini and onion mixture.
Brush an ovenproof baking dish with olive oil. Pour in the egg mixture. Place in the oven for 35–45 minutes or until golden brown on top. Take out of the oven and leave to cool for 10–15 minutes. Cut into large slices and serve with a rocket salad. If zucchini is not your thing, you can substitute any vegetable that you like for the zucchini.

Prep time: 15 minutes
Cooking time: 45–55 minutes
Serves: 4

Utensils:
Oven poor baking dish
Mixing bowls
Fork
Grater

Tuna, Cannellini Bean and Zucchini Triangles

Prep time: 10–15 minutes
Cooking time: 30 minutes
Serves: 4

Utensils:
Baking tray
Mixing bowls
Measuring cups
Measuring spoons

200g (7oz) tinned tuna in spring water (optional)
2 cups grated zucchini
1 small onion, finely chopped
200g (7oz) tin organic cannellini beans, drained and rinsed
2 tablespoons cottage cheese
¼ cup rice, spelt or wholemeal flour
1 egg, lightly beaten
2 egg whites, lightly beaten
2 tablespoons extra virgin olive oil
Sea or vegetable salt to taste

Place tuna, zucchini, onion, cannellini beans, cottage cheese and flour in a large bowl and mix well.

Combine eggs, olive oil and salt and stir into zucchini mixture.

Pour mixture into a greased and lined 17cm x 27cm (6½in x 10½in) lamington tin.

Bake at 180°C (350°F/Gas Mark 4) for 30 minutes or until golden.

Cut into triangles and serve with a salad.

Vegetable Moussaka

2 medium eggplants (with skin), cut into thin rounds
4 zucchinis, sliced thinly lengthways
4 carrots, sliced thinly lengthways

White sauce:
500g (1lb) plain natural yoghurt
50g (1¾oz) parmesan cheese, grated
2 eggs
1 teaspoon nutmeg
1 teaspoon sea salt
1 teaspoon chilli powder
1 teaspoon pepper
1 teaspoon honey

Preheat oven to 160°C (300°F/Gas Mark 2). Bake the eggplant, carrots and zucchinis in the oven for approximately 20 minutes or until soft.
Place all the white sauce ingredients in a mixing bowl and whisk until combined.
Layer the ingredients in a baking tray—eggplant, white sauce, zucchini, white sauce, carrot—until the last layer is the white sauce. Bake in the oven for approximately 25 minutes.
Serve with a baby spinach salad.

Prep time: 30 40 minutes
Cooking time: 20–30 minutes
Serves: 4

Utensils:
2 baking trays
Mixing bowl
Spoons
Whisk

1.4kg (3lb) lean lamb cutlets, excess fat removed
200g (7oz) low fat yoghurt
1 clove garlic, crushed
1 Lebanese cucumber, finely chopped
½ Spanish (red) onion, finely diced
1 tablespoon flat leaf parsley
1 tablespoon chopped mint

Combine all ingredients in a large bowl and leave the lamb to marinate for 30 minutes. Preheat the grill to a medium to hot heat. Remove the lamb cutlets from the marinade and place the lamb cutlets under the grill for 4–5 minutes, turning once. Discard the excesses marinate. Serve with a tomato and rocket salad.

Tzatziki Lamb Cutlets

Prep time: 15 minutes
Cooking time: 6–10 minutes
Serves: 4

Utensils:
Mixing bowls
Lemon juicer
Measuring spoons
Serving plates

Vegetable Samosa Pies with Sweet Potato and Lentil Top

1 tablespoon vegetable oil
1 large onion, chopped
1 teaspoon cumin seeds
½ teaspoon fresh ginger
2 teaspoons mild curry powder
2 garlic cloves, crushed
1 cup peas, frozen or fresh
400g (14oz) tin chopped tomatoes, drained of excess liquid
2 cups sweet potato (yam), peeled and cut into 1cm (½in) cubes
2 tablespoons chopped coriander (cilantro) leaves
1 egg beaten
1 tablespoon lemon juice
Salt and pepper

Sweet potato and lentil top:
1 cup chopped sweet potato (yam)
1 cup cooked lentils
1½ tablespoons sesame seeds
2 tablespoons olive oil

Mango chutney, to serve

Prep time: 15 minutes
Cooking time: 20 minutes
Serves: 6

Utensils:
Sharp knives
One large baking dish or 6 individual ramekins
Frying pan
Mixing bowl

One carrot has enough beta-caotene for the whole day! Carrots help improve the digestive system and lower cholesterol because of their pectin content.

Preheat oven to 180°C (350°F/Gas Mark 4).

Heat the oil in a deep frying pan over medium heat. Add the onion and cook, stirring for 2 minutes or until soft. Add the cumin seeds, ground ginger and curry powder and stir for a minute or until fragrant.

Add the garlic, peas, tomatoes and sweet potato cubes and cook stirring for 10 minutes or until the sweet potato is slightly soft. Stir in coriander and then remove from the heat and set aside.

Stir the egg and lemon juice into the cooled mixture and season to taste.

Place all of the ingredients into a large baking dish or individual ramekins.

To make the topping: Steam the remainder of the sweet potato and once cooked, mash with the cooked lentils, sesame seeds and olive oil. Spread thickly on top of the vegetable mix and bake in the over for 15 minutes or until golden brown on top.

Serve with mango chutney and a green salad.

Warm Asian Chicken and Tofu Salad

1 tablespoon olive oil
200g (7oz) chicken breast, cut into thick strips
200g (7oz) organic hard tofu, chopped into medium-sized cubes
1 cup chopped snow peas (mange tout)
1 cup peas, frozen or fresh
1 capsicum chopped
1 grated carrot
½ cup shredded mint
½ cup shredded coriander (cilantro)

Dressing:
6 tablespoons mirin or 3 tablespoons lemon juice
2 tablespoons miso paste
1½ tablespoons apple cider vinegar
1 small red chilli chopped (to taste)
1 clove garlic, minced
1 teaspoon honey
A little water if needed

Prep time: 20 minutes
Serves: 4

Utensils:
Mixing bowls
Sharp knives
Spoons
Serving bowl

Heat olive oil in a saucepan then cook the chicken breast until golden brown.

In a large bowl, combine the cooked chicken, tofu, snow peas, peas, capsicum, carrot, mint and coriander and mix thoroughly.

To make the dressing: In a small bowl, stir together the mirin, miso, vinegar, chilli, garlic and honey. Pour over the salad and toss to combine.

If you have time, let the salad sit for 30 minutes so the tofu can absorb the flavours of the dressing.

Warm Chicken Salad with Quinoa

Prep time: 10 minutes
Cooking time: 25 minutes
Serves: 4–6

Utensils:
Measuring spoons
2x mixing bowls
Measuring cups
Saucepan

Chicken:
1 tablespoon olive oil
2 x 200g (7oz) chicken breasts, cut into thick strips
1 teaspoon dried marjoram
Salt and pepper to season

Salad:
1 cup quinoa
2 cups water
¼ cup Spanish (red) onion, chopped
½ cup red capsicum, diced
½ cup green capsicum, diced
½ cup chopped fresh basil
1 cup chopped tomato
1 teaspoon garlic, crushed
2 tablespoons apple cider vinegar
3 tablespoons extra virgin olive oil
1 teaspoon fresh chili

Mix all the chicken ingredients together in a bowl to coat chicken. Heat olive oil in a saucepan and cook chicken until golden brown.

Cook the quinoa in a saucepan with the two cups of water: Stir constantly over medium heat about 5 minutes until it just becomes aromatic. Reduce the heat to low, cover the pan and simmer for about 15 minutes. Drain the quinoa if necessary and then transfer it to a large bowl.

Add all the remaining ingredients including the chicken and thoroughly combine with the quinoa. Add salt and pepper to taste and serve immediately.

Prawn and Avocado Salad (see page 178)

Dinner

We have all been told that dinner should be the smallest meal of the day, but one has to be realistic. Dinner can be a healthy size but just make sure you don't overeat. Dinner should be eaten as early as possible simply so you can digest your food and burn part of the energy consumed.

These dinners winners for your waistline. They are delicious, light and will get your taste buds singing.

Asian Stir-fry with Tuna

1 tablespoon sesame oil
2 x 200g (7oz) tuna steaks, cut into thick strips
1 cup bok choy
1 cup Chinese broccoli
½ cup snow peas
1 cup red capsicum, roughly chopped
1 teaspoon red chilli, deseeded and chopped
1 teaspoon ginger, finely grated
1 teaspoon garlic, crushed
4 tablespoons salt-reduced soy sauce
¼ cup roughly chopped fresh mint
¼ cup roughly chopped fresh coriander (cilantro)

In a hot wok, heat the sesame oil and cook tuna until golden brown. Remove from the wok and rest on a plate. Add remaining ingredients to the wok except for coriander and mint. Stir-fry for approximately 5–10 minutes. Add the tuna, mint and coriander and gently mix through. Serve immediately.

Prep time: 10 minutes
Cooking time: 30 minutes
Serves: 2

Utensils:
Wok
Chopping board
Measuring spoons
Serving bowls

Baked Barramundi with Tomato and Basil

Prep time: 15–20 minutes
Cooking time: 20–25 minutes
Serves: 4

Utensils:
Frying pan
Silver foil
Baking tray
Measuring cups
Measuring spoons
Serving plate

4 x 200g (7oz) Barramundi or white fish fillets
Salt and pepper, to season

Tomato and basil sauce:
2 garlic cloves, crushed
1 tablespoon olive oil
1 bunch of fresh parsley, remove from stalk and chopped
400g (14oz) tin of organic tomatoes, chopped
¼ cup balsamic vinegar
Zest from ½ lemon
1 bunch of basil, remove from stalk and chop

To make the sauce: Sauté the garlic in the olive oil in a frying pan, then add the parsley, tomatoes, balsamic vinegar and lemon zest and simmer for approximately 7–10 minutes.

Preheat oven to 160°C (300°F/Gas Mark 2). Season the fish and place flat on a sheet of foil. Generously cover the fillets with the tomato sauce and then sprinkle with the chopped basil. Wrap fish in the foil, making sure the parcel doesn't leak. Place in a baking tray and cook for 15 minutes. Serve with a green salad or vegetable.

2 x 200g (7oz) kingfish, or meaty, textured fish fillet
Olive oil, salt and pepper to season the kingfish
200g (7oz) fresh broad beans
10 cherry tomatoes, halved
4 small radishes sliced in rounds
10 snow peas cut into slices on an angle
½ cup mix lettuce leaves

Tahini dressing:
2 tablespoons tahini
2 tablespoons olive oil
2 tablespoons water
2 tablespoons apple cider vinegar
1 garlic clove crushed
¼ cup parsley
1 teaspoon honey

Season the fish with a little olive oil, sea salt and pepper and pan-fry until slightly pink in the middle, approximately 4–5 minutes on each side. Alternatively bake in the oven at 160°C (300°F/Gas Mark 2).
Mix the broad beans, cherry tomatoes, radishes and snow peas together in a bowl.
In another bowl, whisk together dressing ingredients and then stir into the broad bean salad.
To serve, spoon the ingredients onto a bed of lettuce with the sliced fish on top.

Kingfish with Broad Bean and Tahini Salad

Prep time: 5 minutes
Cooking time: 15 minutes
Serves: 2

Utensils:
2 mixing bowls
Frying pan or baking dish
Knives
Mixing spoons
Whisk
Serving plate

Baked Miso Salmon

Prep time: 30–40 minutes
Cooking time: 20–30 minutes
Serves: 4

Utensils:
Mixing bowls
Baking tray
Serving plate

4 x 100g (3½oz) salmon fillets

Miso marinade:
450g (15½oz) white miso paste
200g (7oz) honey
100g (3½oz) tahini
1 cup rice vinegar
1 cup mirin

To make the marinade: Combine all the ingredients in a bowl and stir well.

Place the salmon in the marinade and leave overnight (do not marinate the fish more than two nights or they will become hard and too salty).

Preheat oven to 170°C (325° F/Gas Mark 3).

Wipe clean the salmon fillets with paper towel and place them on an oiled baking tray.

Bake for 5–7 minutes on each side, or until cooked.

Serve with steamed broccoli.

Beef and Vegetable Moussaka

Moussaka:

1 small onion, chopped thoroughly
1 teaspoon garlic
300g (10oz) lean beef mince (ground beef)
400g (14oz) tin crushed tomatoes
4 medium eggplants (with skin), sliced thinly lengthways
4 zucchinis, sliced thinly lengthways

White sauce:

500g (1lb) low fat natural plain yoghurt
50g (1¾oz) parmesan cheese, grated
2 eggs
1 teaspoon nutmeg
1 teaspoon sea salt
1 teaspoon chilli powder
1 teaspoon pepper

Prep time: 30–40 minutes
Cooking time: 20–30 minutes
Serves: 4

Utensils:
2 baking trays
Saucepan
Mixing bowl
Spoons
Whisk
Serving plates

Sauté the onion and garlic in a saucepan until golden brown. Add the beef mince, stirring, until browned, and then add the tomatoes. Cook a further 10–15 minutes until tomatoes are soft then leave to cool.

Preheat oven to 160°C (300°F/Gas Mark 2). Bake the eggplant and zucchinis in the oven for approximately 15–20 minutes or until soft. Place white sauce ingredients in a mixing bowl and whisk until combined. Layer the ingredients in a baking tray—eggplant, beef mixture, white sauce, zucchini, white sauce—until the last layer is white sauce. Bake in the oven for approximately 25 minutes. Serve with a baby spinach salad.

Beef, Tomato and Pea Curry

1 tablespoon macadamia nut oil or olive oil
1 medium onion, chopped
2 chillies, finely chopped
1 teaspoon cumin seed
1 teaspoon turmeric
2 tablespoons curry powder
400g (14oz) lean blade steak, trimmed and cut into cubes
4 cloves garlic, crushed
2 teaspoons fresh ginger root, crushed
200g (7oz) tin crushed tomatoes
1 cup fresh or frozen peas
1 cup water or beef stock

Heat oil in heavy saucepan and gently fry onion, chilli until onion is golden. Stir in cumin, turmeric and curry powder. Add the beef, brown slightly and cook for 10 minutes, stirring occasionally. Add garlic and ginger, cover and cook for a further 5 minutes. Pour in tinned tomatoes, peas, water or stock. Reduce heat and simmer until the meat is tender. Serve with steamed vegetables.

Prep time: 10 minutes
Cooking time: 30 minutes
Serves: 4

Utensils:
Heavy sauce pan
Measuring cups
Measuring spoons
Sharp knife
Serving bowl or plate

Chicken and Vegetable Millet Pilaf

4 tablespoons olive oil
1 small onion, roughly chopped
1 cup millet (hulled)
1 teaspoon sea salt
1 cup water
½ cup slivered almonds (or sunflower seeds or pepitas)
1 large leek, finely chopped
1 large zucchini, finely chopped
1 bunch asparagus, blanched
400g (14oz) tin crushed tomatoes
2 x 200g (7oz) chicken breasts, cut into strips
1 cup mushrooms
Freshly ground black pepper
¼ teaspoon ground cinnamon

Prep time: 15 minutes
Cooking time: 30 minutes
Serves: 2

Utensils:
Sharp knives
Large frying pan
Mixing bowl
Serving plates

Heat 2 teaspoons of the oil in a saucepan and sauté the onion for about 3 minutes until tender but not brown. Add the millet and cook for another 2 minutes or so stirring occasionally. Sprinkle in the salt and pour in the water. Bring to the boil, lower heat and simmer covered for about 20 minutes. Set aside.
Place the almonds under a grill and toast until lightly browned, turning frequently. Set aside. Heat the remaining 2 teaspoons of oil in a frying pan and add the tinned tomatoes, finely chopped leek and zucchini and chicken strips. Stir-fry for about 7–10 minutes. Slice the mushrooms thinly and add them to the chicken and vegetable mixture. Stir-fry for a further 2–3 minutes. When the millet is tender and the water is absorbed, stir in the chicken and vegetables, and add pepper and cinnamon to taste. Cook for a further 2 minutes, stirring, then remove from the heat and stir in the almonds and asparagus. Serve immediately.

155

Chicken Breast with Roast Vegetables

Prep time: 20–25 minutes
Cooking time: 15 minutes
Serves: 2

Utensils:
Mixing bowl
Roasted pan
Saucepan
Sharp knives
Serving plate

2 x 200g (7oz) chicken breasts
1 tablespoon olive oil
1 teaspoon dried rosemary
1 teaspoon garlic
1 teaspoon sea salt

Roast vegetables:
1 red pepper
1 green pepper
2 red onions
2 zucchinis
1 large field mushroom
1 punnet of cherry tomatoes
6 garlic gloves, skins removed
3 tablespoon extra virgin olive oil
3 tablespoons fresh thyme (basil and parsley also work well)
¼ cup water
Sea salt and pepper

Place all the chicken ingredients into a bowl and marinate for 20 minutes.

Preheat oven to 180°C (350°F/Gas Mark 4).
Slice all the vegetables and mushroom into 1cm (½in) rounds, leaving the tomatoes and garlic whole.

Toss all the vegetables and garlic together in a large roasting pan with the olive oil, thyme, ¼ cup water, salt and pepper. Place in oven for 15–20 minutes or until the vegetables are soft.

In a frying pan, heat a little olive oil and once the pan is hot add the chicken breast and cook for about 10 minutes, turning once.

Serve the chicken on a bed of the roast vegetables.

2 tablespoons light soy sauce
2 tablespoons sake
2 tablespoons mirin
2 tablespoons light miso
2 spring onions, thinly sliced
1 teaspoon freshly grated ginger
1 garlic clove, crushed
8 chicken thighs
1 teaspoon sesame seeds

Place the soy sauce, sake, mirin, miso, onions, ginger and garlic in a bowl and mix well. Add the chicken pieces, turn to coat well and marinate at room temperature for 1 hour, turning several times.
Preheat grill to very hot.
Remove the chicken from the marinade and pat dry on kitchen paper. Grill for 5 minutes then turn chicken and grill for a further 5 minutes or until brown and cooked through.
Serve with a sprinkle of sesame seeds and steamed Chinese broccoli.

Grilled Miso Chicken

Prep time: 20 minutes
Cooking time: 10 minutes
Serves: 4

Utensils:
Mixing bowl
Serving plate

Citrus Marinated Salmon with Vegetable Salad

Salad:

1 cup grated carrot
1 cup cos (romaine) lettuce, washed and shredded
½ cup chopped capsicum
¼ cup finely chopped parsley
¼ cup finely chopped coriander (cilantro)
1 Spanish (red) onion, roughly chopped

Dressing:

1 teaspoon lemon juice
1 tablespoon orange juice
1 teaspoon lime juice
1 tablespoon tamari
1 teaspoon fresh ginger
2 garlic cloves
2 tablespoons olive oil
1 teaspoon fresh chilli, deseeded and finely chopped

Marinade:

1 tablespoon lemon juice
1 teaspoon lemon zest
1 tablespoon lime juice
1 teaspoon lime zest
1 tablespoon orange juice
1 teaspoon orange zest

4 x 150g–200g (5oz–7oz) salmon fillet
1–2 tablespoons sheep's milk yoghurt

Prep time: 20 minutes
Cooking time: 5–8 minutes
Serves: 4

Utensils:
Chopping board
Mixing bowl
Small bowl for ingredients
Frying pan
Measuring spoons
Lemon juicer
Lemon zester
Grater

To make the salad: Mix the carrots, lettuce, capsicum, parsley, coriander and Spanish onion in a serving bowl.

Whisk together the lemon, orange and lime juice, tamari, ginger, garlic and chilli. Pour over the salad and combine well.

Combine the marinade ingredients in a bowl. Add the salmon and marinate for 10 minutes.

Lightly pan-fry the salmon until slightly pink in the middle.

Serve the salmon on a bed of the salad with a dollop of sheep's milk yoghurt.

Stir-fried Pork with Lentils and Spinach

1 cup red lentils
1 tablespoon olive oil
2 garlic cloves, crushed
½ teaspoons ground cumin
½ teaspoons sweet paprika
500g (1lb) English spinach, stalks removed
¼ cup chopped fresh coriander (cilantro), and extra to serve
¼ cup chopped fresh parsley, and extra to serve
Salt and pepper
⅓ cup plain soy yoghurt (optional)

Place the lentils in a pan with 2 cups (500ml/1 pint) hot water and a generous pinch of sea salt. Cover partially, bring to the boil, then reduce the heat and simmer for 15 minutes, or until the lentils are tender. Drain well.

Heat the olive oil in a large frying pan. Add the garlic and spices and stir for 2 minutes, then add the spinach. When the spinach wilts, add the lentils, coriander and parsley, and stir-fry until the lentils are heated through. Season with salt and freshly ground black pepper. To serve, top with soy yoghurt and garnish with the extra herbs.

Prep time: 15–20 minutes
Cooking time: 20–25 minutes
Serves: 4

Utensils:
Measuring spoons
Measuring bowls
Sauce pan
Frying pan
Serving plate

Eye Fillet with Walnut Rosemary Quinoa

Prep time: 15 minutes
Cooking time: 15–30 minutes
Serves: 4

Utensils:
Frying pan
Saucepan
Measuring cups
Serving plates

1kg (2lb) beef eye fillet
1 tablespoon sesame oil
1 small onion
1½ cups quinoa, rinsed in boiling water and drained
1 small red pepper, diced
3 cups water
1 tablespoon tamari (or to taste)
2 teaspoons fresh or dried rosemary
½ cup walnuts, chopped

Preheat oven to 180°C (350°F/Gas Mark 4).

Heat a little olive oil in a medium saucepan. Sear the beef on each side for about one minute and then place in the oven for 15 minutes. Once cooked, take it out of the oven, cover with foil and rest it for 5–10 minutes.

Heat sesame oil in a medium saucepan then add onion and quinoa. Sauté the mixture over medium heat, stirring constantly, for about 3 minutes. Add red pepper and sauté an additional 2 minutes.

Add water, soy sauce, rosemary and peas (if using fresh peas). Bring to the boil and cover. Simmer for 15 minutes or until water is absorbed.

Meanwhile, roast the walnuts in oven for 5 to 10 minutes. When quinoa is cooked, turn off heat and mix in walnuts. Let the quinoa sit for an additional 10 minutes and then serve.

To serve place the eye fillet whole, on top of a bad of the walnut rosemary quinoa.

Grilled Tuna with Ligurian Olive and Basil Tapenade

Prep time: 15 minutes
Cooking time: 15 minutes
Serves: 5

Utensils:
Food processor
Mixing bowl
Measuring cups
Serving plate

4 x 200g (7oz) tuna steaks
Salt and pepper to taste
2 tablespoons olive oil

Tapenade:
1 large red capsicum, seeds remove and chopped
1 cup Ligurian olives, pips removed
½ cup shredded basil
2 tablespoons lemon juice
¼ cup olive oil

Preheat the barbecue. Brush the tuna with the olive oil and season with salt and pepper. Leave to sit for 10–15 minutes.

Place all the tapenade ingredients in a food processor and blend until smooth.

Cook tuna on the barbecue for 3–5 minutes each side, until just pink inside.

Serve the tuna steaks with a generous spoonful of the tapenade and a salad on the side.

Turkey and Vegetable Soup

8 cups water
4 tablespoons miso paste
400g (14oz) tin crushed tomatoes
2 carrots, sliced
1 small head cabbage, shredded
1kg (2lb) turkey mince (ground turkey)
1 cup button mushrooms, sliced
1 cup pearl barley
1 cup fresh mixed herbs

In a large saucepan, combine water, miso paste, tomatoes, carrots, mushrooms and cabbage. Bring to a boil. Turn heat down and let simmer. In a heavy-based frying pan, brown the turkey. Once cooked, place it in the saucepan with the other ingredients. Simmer for an hour. Add barley and herbs for the last 15 minutes of cooking time. Ladle into bowls and serve hot.

Prep time: 15 minutes
Cooking time: 1 hour and 15 minutes
Serves: 5 people

Utensils:
Heavy-based frying pan
Measuring cups
Measuring spoons
Sharp knife
Serving bowls

Lactose-free Chicken Boscaiola

Prep time: 5 minutes
Cooking time: 15 minutes
Serves: 2

Utensils:
2 frying pans
Knives
Serving plate

2 x 200g (7oz) chicken breasts
3 tablespoons olive oil
1 tablespoon marjoram, fresh or dried

Boscaiola sauce:
½ Spanish (red) onion, chopped finely
2 garlic cloves, crushed
2 cups mixed mushrooms (shiitake, field, and porcini mushrooms), chopped
¼ cup roughly chopped flat leaf parsley
¼ cup roughly chopped basil
1 tablespoon lemon zest
1 teaspoon fresh chilli, chopped
1 tablespoon lemon juice
3 tablespoons low-fat soy mayonnaise (optional)
200ml (6½oz) natural soy yoghurt

Coat the chicken breast in olive oil and marjoram and marinate for 10 minutes. Pan-fry the chicken in a hot frying pan for 5 minutes each side.

To make the boscaiola sauce: Sauté the onion, garlic and mushrooms in a little olive oil. Add the parsley, basil, lemon zest, chilli and lemon juice. Pour in the soy mayonnaise and soy yoghurt and stir over a medium heat for 10–15 minutes.

Plate the chicken and pour a generous amount of the boscaiola sauce over the top. Serve with a simple green salad.

4 x 200g (7oz) lamb backstraps
Salt and pepper
1 tablespoon olive oil
1 teaspoon lemon juice
100g (3½oz) mozzarella cheese, grated

Tomato sauce:
375g (13oz) ripe fresh tomatoes
2–3 tablespoons olive oil
Bunch fresh basil leaves, roughly torn
1 teaspoon fresh oregano
3 tablespoons freshly grated parmesan cheese

To make the sauce: Skin and finely chop the tomatoes. Put in a bowl with the olive oil, basil leaves, oregano and grated parmesan cheese. Leave to marinate for 30 minutes then cook in a hot frying pan for 5 minutes.
Brush the backstraps with the olive oil and lemon juice and season to taste. Preheat the barbecue or a skillet pan. Barbecue or fry lamb for 4 minutes each side or until medium to rare. Place meat on serving plates and sprinkle the mozzarella over the top and let it melt slightly. Pour the hot tomato sauce over the top. Serve with steamed green beans.

Lamb Backstrap with Mozzarella, Tomato and Parmesan Sauce

Prep time: 20 minutes
Cooking time: 15 minutes
Serves: 4

Utensils:
Skillet pan or barbecue
2 mixing bowls
Grater
Measuring spoons
Serving plates

Lamb Backstraps with African Millet Salad

Prep time: 15–20
Cooking time: 20–25
Serves: 2

Utensils:
Saucepan
Measuring spoons
Juicer
Mixing bowl
Serving plates
Knifes

Lamb:
2 lamb backstraps
1 tablespoon olive oil
1 tablespoon lemon juice
Sea salt to taste

Millet salad:
¾ cup millet
2–3 cups water
1 small onion, chopped
1 garlic clove, crushed
1½ teaspoons fresh ginger
1½ teaspoons cumin
1½ teaspoons smoked paprika
¼ cup raw pistachio nuts
¼ cup currants
½ cup coriander (cilantro)

Brush the backstraps with the olive oil and lemon juice and season to taste. Leave to marinate for 10 minutes.

Place the millet and water in a saucepan and cook until tender or until all the water has been absorbed; approximately 15–20 minutes

Sauté onion, garlic and ginger until gold brown. Add the cumin, smoked paprika and cooked millet and mix through. Add pistachio nuts, currants and coriander. Spoon into a bowl and drizzle a little olive oil over the top.

Preheat the barbecue or a skillet pan to a medium to high heat and cook the backstrap for 4 minutes each side or until medium to rare.

Serve lamb sliced over a bed of African millet salad. Garnish with mint or coriander to serve.

 Tip

Include a good source of meat or vegetarian protein with each meal. You should eat 1g of meat protein per kg of your body weight. Eg. 75g of protein is recommended for a weight of 75kg.

Mediterranean Lamb Burgers

Prep time: 10–15 minutes
Cooking time: 10
Makes 4 burgers

Utensils:
Frying pan
3 mixing bowls
Measuring cups
Measuring spoons
Serving plate

Yoghurt sauce:
200g (7oz) plain low fat yogurt
1 garlic clove, crushed
¼ teaspoon sea salt
3 teaspoon fresh mint leaves, shredded

Burgers:
1kg (2lb) lamb mince (ground lamb), from the shoulder
1 garlic clove, crushed
1 tablespoon chopped fresh rosemary
1 tablespoon chopped fresh parsley
Salt and pepper to taste

Salad:
$^1/_3$ cup kalamata olives, seeded and coarsely chopped
2 ripe medium tomatoes, coarsely chopped
3 tablespoons chopped fresh parsley
2 tablespoons olive oil
2 tablespoons apple cider vinegar
¼ cup low fat feta or goat's cheese, crumbled (optional)
6 wholemeal pita bread, split in half

Combine the yoghurt ingredients into a bowl and mix thoroughly. Set aside.

Preheat the barbecue or a frying pan and brush with a little olive oil. Combine all the lamb ingredients in a bowl and cook in the frying pan for 6 minutes each side, or until medium to rare.

To make the salad, combine olives, tomatoes, parsley, olive oil and apple cider vinegar in a bowl. Season with salt and pepper.

Transfer burgers to pita pockets and sprinkle with feta or goat's cheese. Serve with yoghurt sauce and salad.

For a no-carbohydrates option, serve the burger with yoghurt sauce and the salad on the side, without the bread.

☞ **Tip**

Make a shopping list on Sunday or Monday morning and buy the food you will need for your meals and snacks for the week.

4 x 200g (7oz) pork cutlets, all fat trimmed off
Salt and pepper

Tofu dressing:
1 cup silken tofu (you can also use avocado)
2 tablespoons olive oil
3 cloves garlic
1 teaspoon honey or agave nectar
½ teaspoons pepper
4 tablespoon fresh lemon juice
1 tablespoon miso paste
½ teaspoons fresh herbs
Water to thin if necessary

Preheat the grill or barbecue to medium-hot. Cook the pork cutlets for approximately 4–5 minutes each side. Season with salt and pepper. Blend all the tofu ingredients in a food processor until smooth. Serve the pork with the tofu dressing poured over the top and steamed vegetables.

Grilled Pork Cutlets with Tofu Dressing

Prep time: 10–15 minutes
Cooking time: 8–10
Serves: 4

Utensils:
Food processor
Serving plate
Measuring spoons

Prawn and Avocado Salad

Prep time: 30–40 minutes
Cooking time: 10 minutes
Serves: 4

Utensils:
Baking tray
Saucepan
Mixing bowls
Measuring spoons
Zester

150g (5oz) snow peas, washed and trimmed
1 large iceberg lettuce, washed
50g (1¾oz) rocket leaves, washed
50g (1¾oz) snow pea sprouts, washed and trimmed
1 cup mushrooms, sliced
200g (7oz) cherry tomatoes (mixed red and yellow), halved
1kg (2lb) cooked king prawns, peeled, deveined, tails left intact
1 large ripe avocado, chopped
Freshly ground black pepper

Dressing:
2 tablespoons lime juice
1 teaspoon lime zest
2 tablespoons fresh dill, chopped
1 tablespoons tomato sauce, reduced salt (good quality)
2 tablespoons rice wine vinegar
1 teaspoon Liquid Amino or soy sauce

Bring a medium-sized saucepan of water to the boil. Blanch the snow peas until just tender, rinse under cold water and drain well.

Pull off whole lettuce leafs to make little bowls and place onto individual plates. Top with rocket and snow pea sprouts. Arrange snow peas, tomatoes and mushrooms on top of the greens, and then top with prawns and chopped avocado. Season with pepper.

To make the dressing: Place all the ingredients in a bowl and mix thoroughly. Pour the dressing over the salad and serve immediately.

Tuna Patties

1 x 400g (14oz) tin tuna, drained and flaked
½ cup buckwheat fine
½ cup celery, chopped
¼ cup tahini
¼ cup finely chopped onion
2 tablespoons chilli
1 egg, beaten slightly
1 teaspoon sea salt
2 tablespoons olive oil

Mix all ingredients except olive oil in a bowl, and form into four patties.
Heat olive oil in a frying pan over medium heat.
Fry patties until nicely browned; about 5 minutes each side.
Serve with a salad or vegetables.

Prep time: 10–15 minutes
Cooking time: 10
Makes 4 patties

Utensils:
Mixing bowl
Frying pan
Measuring spoons
Serving plate

☞ Tip

Avocado is a healthy source of essential fatty acides and monounsaturated fats, which are extremely important in a child's mental development. Avocado does not increase cholesterol levels.

Prawns with Yoghurt and Lime

Prep time: 15–20 minutes
Cooking time: 20–25 minutes
Serves: 4

Utensils:
BBQ or frying pan
Mixing bowl
Measuring spoons
Serving plate

450g (15½oz) large prawns, shelled
1 tablespoon ginger, crushed
1 garlic clove, crushed
1 teaspoon garam masala
½ teaspoon chilli powder
1 tablespoon group coriander (cilantro)
1 lime zested
1 tablespoon lime juice
125ml (4oz) low fat natural plain yoghurt

Place the prawns on four skewers. Combine all other ingredients in a bowl and mix thoroughly. Put the prawns in the bowl and leave to marinate for 20 minutes.

Preheat the barbecue or a frying pan and brush with a little olive oil. Lightly cook the prawn skewers until they turn pink; approximately 5 minutes each side.

Serve with steamed Chinese vegetables.

Sesame-crusted Kingfish with Lentil Salad

1 teaspoon rice wine vinegar
4 x 200g (7oz) kingfish fillets or a meaty, textured fish fillet
2 tablespoons sesame oil
1 tablespoon black sesame seeds
1 tablespoon white sesame seeds
1 tablespoon sea salt
1 tablespoon pepper

Lentil salad:
400g (14oz) tin organic lentils, washed and drained
¼ cup shallots, chopped
1 garlic clove, crushed
1 teaspoon finely grated fresh ginger
1 tablespoon walnut oil
¼ cup extra virgin olive oil
½ teaspoon cumin
½ teaspoon coriander (cilantro)
½ teaspoon cayenne pepper
½ teaspoon paprika
Zest of ½ lemon

Prep time: 15–20 minutes
Cooking time: 10 minutes
Serves: 4

Utensils:
Frying pan
Mixing bowls
Measuring cups
Measuring spoons
Sharp knives
Serving plate

Mix together all the lentil ingredients and marinate for 30–45 minutes. Brush the fish fillets with the rice wine vinegar. Mix together the sesame oil and sesame seeds and pour over the kingfish. Season with salt and pepper. Preheat the frying pan and brush with a little olive oil, then cook the fish over a medium to hot heat for 5 minutes on each side. Be gentle when turning as the sesame seeds may fall off. Slice the fillets or leave whole and serve with the lentil salad.

Stir-fried Beef with Vegetables and Raw Cashews

1 tablespoon sesame oil
800g (1¾lb) rump steak, cut into thick strips
1 tablespoon ginger, julienne
1 clove garlic
1 small red chilli
1 onion, cup into rounds
1 tablespoon miso paste added to ½ cup of water
1 tablespoon tamari
1 bunch of Chinese broccoli, wash and cut the bunch in half
10 baby corn, cut in half lengthways
200g (7oz) button mushrooms, sliced
½ red capsicum, seeded and sliced
¼ cup raw cashews
1 bunch of coriander (cilantro), chopped, to garnish

Heat a wok or frying pan over medium to high heat. Heat the sesame oil then add the beef, ginger, garlic, chilli, onion, miso and tamari. Stir-fry for 5–10 minutes. Add all the vegetables and cashews and cook for a further 5–7 minutes. Be careful not to overcook; you still want the vegetables to be crunchy. Serve topped with coriander.

Prep time: 20 minutes
Cooking time: 15 minutes
Serves: 4

Utensils:
Work or frying pan
Sharp knife
Measuring spoons
Measuring cups
Serving plate

Tofu Lettuce Burgers

Prep time: 10–15 minutes
Cooking time: 8–10
Serves: 4

Utensils:
Frying pan
Mixing bowl
Measuring cups
Measuring spoons
Serving plates

1 onion, finely chopped
1 garlic clove, crushed
2 tablespoons olive oil
1 cup hard tofu, crumbled
½ to 1 cup of wholemeal breadcrumbs
2 eggs, cracked
½ cup carrot, finely grated
2 tablespoons Worcestershire sauce
½ teaspoon sea salt
1 teaspoon pepper
4 large cos (romaine) lettuce leaves, wash and dried
1 tomato, sliced

Sauté the garlic and onion in a frying pan in 1 tablespoon of olive oil until a light golden brown.

Place the onion mixture into a mixing bowl and then add all the remaining ingredients apart from the lettuce and tomato, and mix thoroughly.

Shape the mixture into 4 burgers.

Heat the remaining olive oil in the frying pan. Place the tofu burgers into the frying pan and cook for 4–5 minutes on each side.

Serve the burgers in the lettuce with a little tomato.

Trout with Creamy Avocado Sauce and Asparagus

4 x 200g (7oz) trout fillets
1 tablespoon olive oil
1 tablespoon lemon juice
Salt and pepper to season
2 bunches of asparagus, ends trimmed off

Avocado sauce:
2 ripe avocados, chopped
Juice of 1 lemon
1 garlic clove, chopped
1 tablespoon olive oil
1 tablespoon low fat natural plain yoghurt
1 teaspoon honey

To make avocado sauce: Place all ingredients in a food processor and pulse until a creamy consistency. Preheat a frying pan. Brush fillets with olive oil and lemon juice and season. Place fillets in medium to hot frying pan and cook for 5 minutes each side. Bring a saucepan of water to the boil, add asparagus and cook for 5 minutes. Be careful not to overcook; you want them to be slightly crunchy. To serve, place the trout on a plate with the asparagus at the side and then spoon over the avocado sauce. Garnish with a sprig of parsley.

Prep time: 5–10 minutes
Cooking time:
Serves: 4

Utensils:
Food processor
Saucepan
Frying pan
Spoons
Mixing bowl
Juicer
Serving plate

Turkey with Five-flavours Sauces

4 x 200–250g (7oz–8oz) lean turkey breasts
¼ cup olive oil
2 spring onions, minced
2½ tablespoons soy sauce
2½ tablespoons brown sugar
2 garlic cloves, crushed
1 tablespoon sesame oil

Combine all ingredients in a mixing bowl and leave to marinate for 40 minutes.
Preheat oven to 180°C (350°F/Gas Mark 4).
Wrap the individual turkey breasts in baking paper or silver foil and place in a baking tray. Cook for 20 minutes.
Serve with stir-fried vegetables.

Prep time: 15–20 minutes
Cooking time: 20–25 minutes
Serves: 4

Utensils:
Silver foil
Baking tray
Measuring spoons
Serving plate

Veal with Braised Fennel and Garlic

Prep time: 15 minutes
Cooking time: 20–25 minutes
Serves: 4

Utensils:
Mixing bowls
Deep frying pan
Sharp knife
Frying pan
Measuring spoons
Serving plates

Veal:
4 x 200g (7oz) veal loin steaks or veal chops
1 tablespoon lemon juice
1 tablespoon olive oil

Fennel and garlic:
2 tablespoons olive oil
2 bulbs fennel, cut into quarters
6 cloves of garlic
¼ cup water
1 teaspoon dried basil
1 teaspoon dried parsley
½ teaspoon sea salt
½ teaspoon pepper

In a deep frying pan, sauté the olive oil, fennel and garlic until lightly browned. Stir in the water and herbs. Cover and simmer over low heat for 10–15 minute or until soft.

Preheat another frying pan. Brush the veal with the lemon juice, olive oil, pepper and salt, then place in the frying pan and cook for 3 minutes on each side.

Serve the veal with fennel on the side.

Sweets and Treats

You would not be human if you did not want to have a sweet treat every now and then. But you don't need to eat sugar. There are sugar-free alternatives and it's okay now and then to have a naughty treat.

Agave Sugar-free Banana Muffins

2 cups wholemeal flour
2 teaspoons baking powder
¼ cup almond meal
¼ cup olive oil (optional)
2 eggs
1½ cups soy milk
½ cup agave nectar
2 bananas mashed
½ cup oats
1 tablespoon cinnamon

Sift all dry ingredients, except oats, and mix together thoroughly. Add all wet ingredients and mix thoroughly. Add oats and mix well. Spray a muffin tray with olive oil spray and spoon mixture in. Bake at 160°C (300F°/Gas Mark 2) for 25–30 minutes or until golden. Enjoy with a cup of chamomile tea.

Prep time: 10–15 minutes
Cooking time: 15–20 minutes
Makes 8–10 muffins

Utensils:
Measuring cups
Mixing bowl
Muffin tin

☞ Tip

Instead of chocolates or lollies; try eating organic dried fruits, such as apricots. Apricots give you the sugar hit without making you feel tired. They also help to prevent obesity.

1 tablespoon almonds
1 tablespoon sunflower
1 tablespoon sesame seeds
1 tablespoon pepitas
1 tablespoon walnuts
1 punnet strawberries
1 tablespoon honey
1 teaspoon cinnamon
1 cup goat's milk yoghurt

Preheat oven to 120°C (250°F/Gas Mark ½). Place all the nuts on an oven tray and bake for 5–10 minutes or until slightly golden brown.
Place the strawberries, honey and cinnamon in a blender or food processor and blend until smooth.
To serve, divide the yoghurt between two serving bowls, pour the strawberry puree over the top then sprinkle with the nuts.

Toasted Nuts with Strawberry Puree and Yoghurt

Prep time: 10–15 minutes
Serves: 2

Utensils:
Oven tray
Blender
Decorative serving bowls

Roasted Coconut and Spring Fruit Salad

Prep time: 15minutes
Cooking time: 5
Serves: 2–4

Utensils:
Food processor
Baking tray
Juicer
Mixing bowls
Sharp knives
Serving bowls

100g (3½oz) coconut slivers
½ cup chopped paw-paw
½ cup chopped pear
½ cup chopped mangoes
1 orange cut into segments

Fruit salad dressing:
2 ripe bananas
½ a lemon juice
½ a lime juice
¼ cup mint

Preheat oven to 180°C (350°F/Gas Mark 4). Place the coconut in a baking tray and bake for 5–10 minute or until golden brown.

To make the dressing: Place the banana, lemon juice, lime juice and mint in a blender or food processor and blend until smooth.

In a separate bowl, gently mix together the pawpaw, pears, mangoes and orange segments.

Place the fruit mixture into individual bowls and then pour the fruit salad dressing over the top.

Sprinkle with coconut to finish and serve.

Carob Delight Cookies

Prep time: 15–20 minutes
Makes approximately 20 cookies

Utensils:
Food processor
Spoons
Mixing bowl
Tray
Airtight container

6 dried figs, diced, hard stalk removed (organic)
1 cup walnuts
½ cup macadamia nuts
½ cup brazil nuts
½ cup sunflower seeds
1½ tablespoons honey
⅓ cup carob powder
½ cup raspberries
1 cup LSA (linseed, almonds and sunflower seeds)

Combine all ingredients except the carob powder, the raspberries and half a cup of LSA in a food processor until coarse and slightly sticky.

Add the carob powder a little at a time until dough is firm.

Take a bit of the dough, put a raspberry in the centre, and form into a 2.5cm (1in) ball around the raspberry.

Roll the ball in the remaining LSA to coat. Continue until all the mixture is rolled.

Store cookies in the refrigerator in an airtight container.

Summer Berry Guilt-free Ice-cream

2 cups of frozen mixed berries
3 bananas cut into 2cm rounds and frozen
1 teaspoon cinnamon
1 teaspoon nutmeg
1 teaspoon agave nectar
2 tablespoons fresh mint leaves

Place all the ingredients into a food process and pulse until an ice-cream consistency.
Server in either a martini glass or a glass bowl

Prep time: 10minutes
Serves: 2-4

 Tip

Strawberries help to increase bowel motions and reduce serum cholesterol levels. You can even mash and apply to your teeth to whiten them!

Weights and Measures

The conversions given in the recipes in this book are approximate. The exact equivalents in the following tables have been rounded for convenience.

Dry Weights

Grams (g)	Ounces (oz)
1	30
2	60
3	90
4	125
5	150
6	180
7	200
8	250
10	300
14	400
500g	1lb
1kg	2lb
1.5kg	3lb

 Tip

Healthy weight loss is approximately 500g (1lb) per week. Losing weight fast can slow your Basal Metabolic Rate (BMR), resulting in stationary metabolism

Liquids

Cups/Tablespoons	Fluid Ounces	Millilitres
2 tablespoons	1 fl oz	30ml
¼ cup (4 tablespoons)	2 fl oz	60ml
⅓ cup	3 fl oz	80ml
½ cup	4 fl oz	125ml
⅔ cup	5 fl oz	160ml
¾ cup	6 fl oz	180ml
1 cup	8 fl oz	250ml
1¼ cups	10 fl oz	300ml
1½ cups	12 fl oz	375ml
2 cups	16 fl oz	500ml
	2 pints	1 litre
	3 pints	3.5 litres
	5 pints	2.5 litres

Oven Temperatures

Gas Mark	Fahrenheit	Celsius	Description
¼	225	110	Very cool/very slow
½	250	130	---
1	275	140	Cool
2	300	150	---
3	325	170	Very moderate
4	350	180	Moderate
5	375	190	---
6	400	200	Moderately hot
7	425	220	Hot
8	450	230	---
9	475	240	Very hot

Glycemic Index and Fat Content of Common Foods

Bakery foods	GI	Fat
Cake, angel food 30g (1oz)	67	trace
Cake, banana 80g (2½oz)	47	7
Cake, chocolate fudge 78g (2½oz)	38	17
Cake, flan 80g (2½oz)	65	5
Cake, French vanilla 78g (2½oz)	42	15
Cake, pound 80g (2½oz)	54	15
Cake, sponge 40g (1½oz)	66	4
Croissant, 1	67	14
Crumpet 50g (1½oz)	69	0
Cupcakes with icing 38g (1½oz)	73	3
Donut with cinnamon sugar 40g (1½oz)	76	8
Lamingtons, 50g (1½oz)	87	8
Muffin, apple, sultana 50g (1½oz)	54	4
Muffin, apricot 50g (1½oz)	60	4
Muffin, banana	65	4
Muffin, banana, oat, honey 50g (1½oz)	65	4
Muffin, blueberry 80g (2½oz)	59	8
Muffin, bran 80g (2½oz)	60	8
Muffin, chocolate 80g (2½oz)	53	4
Muffins, apple 80g (2½oz)	44	10
Pastry, flaky 65g (2oz)	59	26
Pizza, cheese & tomato 2 slices	60	27
Pizza, supreme 2 slices 2 slices	36	31
Scones, 40g (1½oz)	92	2
Waffles, 25g (¾oz)	76	3

Beverages	GI	Fat
Apple juice 250ml (8fl oz)	40	0
Cola, 250ml (8fl oz)	63	0
Cordial, orange in water 250ml (8fl oz)	66	0
Cranberry juice 250ml (8fl oz)	52	0
Orange soda 250ml (8fl oz)	59	0
Fruit cocktail 250ml (8fl oz)	69	0
Grapefruit juice unsweet 250ml (8fl oz)	48	0
Electrolyte drinking powder, 1 tbsp	95	0
Chocolate drinking powder 1 tbsp	55	2
Strawberry drinking powder 1 tbsp	50	0
Orange cordial 250ml (8fl oz)	66	0
Orange juice 250ml (8fl oz)	46	0
Pineapple juice 250ml (8fl oz)	46	0
Soy milk, light 250ml (8fl oz)	44	4
Soy milk, original 250ml (8fl oz)	44	7

Breads	GI	Fat
Bagel, white 70g (2¼oz)	72	1
Barley flour bread 70g (2¼oz)	35	2
Burgen fruit & muesli 40g (1½oz)	53	2
Burgen oat & honey 40g (1½oz)	49	2
Burgen Rye 40g (1½oz)	51	2
Burgen soy linseed 40g (1½oz)	36	4
Burgen Mixed Grain	52	2
Dark rye, black bread 50g (1½oz)	76	1
English muffin 30g (1oz)	77	1
French baguette 30g (1oz)	95	1
Fruit loaf 35g (1.15oz)	54	1

Fruit n' spice (buttercup) 72g (2¼oz)	54	3
Gluten-free bread 30g (1oz)	90	1
Gluten-free missed grain 40g (1½oz)	79	2
Hamburger bun 50g (1½oz)	61	3
Helga's classic seed 90g (3oz)	68	4
Hyfibre wholemeal 33g (1oz)	46	1
Kaiser rolls 50g (1½oz)	73	1
Lebanese, white 110g (3¾oz)	73	3
Light rye 50g (1½oz)	68	1
Linseed rye 50g (1½oz)	55	5
Melba, toast 60g (2oz)	70	1
Multigrain bread (Tip Top) 30g (1oz)	43	1
Performaz, country loaf 37g (1¼oz)	38	2
Pita bread, white 65g (2.15oz)	57	1
Ploughmans loaf mixed grain 45g (1½oz)	47	1
Ploughmans loaf wholemeal 45g (1½oz)	64	2
Pumpernickel 60g (2oz)	41	1
Riga sunflower & Barley 40g (1½oz)	92	1
Rye bread 50g (1½oz)	65	1
Semolina bread 40g (1½oz)	92	2
Sourdough, rye 30g (1oz)	48	1
Sourdough, wheat 30g (1oz)	54	1
Stone ground wholemeal 30g (1oz)	53	1
Vogel honey & oat 40g (1½oz)	55	3
White, wheat flour 30g (1oz)	70	1
Wholemeal 35g (1.15oz)	69	1
Wonder White 35g (1.15oz)	80	1

Breakfast cereals	GI	Fat
All-Bran, 40g (1½oz)	42	1
All-Bran, fruit n' oats 45g(1½oz)	39	2
All-Bran, soy n' fibre 45g(1½oz)	33	1
Bran Buds w/ psyllium 30g (1oz)	58	0
Bran Flakes 30g (1oz)	74	1
Breakfast Bar, all approximately 30g (1oz)	78	1
Cheerios 30g (1oz)	74	2
Coco Pops 30g (1oz)	77	0
Corn Bran 30g (1oz)	75	1
Corn Chex 30g (1oz)	83	0
Corn Flakes 30g (1oz)	84	0
Crunchy Nut Cornflakes 30g (1oz)	72	1
Fruit Loops 30g (1oz)	69	1
Golden Wheats, 30g (1oz)	71	0
Guardian 30g (1oz)	42	0
Healthwise for bowl 45g (1½oz)	66	1
Healthwise for heart 45g(1½oz)	48	3
Honey Rice Bubbles 30g (1oz)	77	0
Honey Smacks 30g (1oz)	56	1
Just Right Just Grains 45g(1½oz)	62	1
Just Right 30g (1oz)	60	1
Komplete Oven Bake 45g (1½oz)	48	3
Mini-Wheat Whole Wheat 30g (1oz)	58	0
Mini-Wheat Blackcurrant 30g (1oz)	71	0
Muesli non-toasted 60g (2oz)	56	6
Muesli, gluten-free 40g (1½oz)	39	12
Nutri-Grain 30g (1oz)	66	0
Oats Bran, raw 2 teaspoons	55	1
Oat n' Honey bake 45g (1½oz)	77	6

	GI	Fat
Porridge cooked w/ water 60g (2oz)	42	2
Puffed Wheat 30g (1oz)	80	1
Rice Bran, extruded 2 teaspoons	19	2
Popped Rice 30g (1oz)	82	0
Rice chex 30g (1oz)	89	0
Rice Krispies 30g (1oz)	82	0
Rolled oats cooked w. water 60g (2oz)	42	2
Semolina, cooked 60g (2oz)	55	0
Shredded Wheat 1 tablespoon	67	0
Special K 30g (1oz)	54	0
Sultana Bran 45g (1½oz)	73	1
Sustain 30g (1oz)	68	1
Team 30g (1oz)	82	0
Total 30g (1oz)	76	0
Vita Brits 30g (1oz)	61	1
Weet-Bix 30g (1oz)	69	1
Wheatbites 30g (1oz)	72	1

Cereal grains

	GI	Fat
Barley, pearled boiled 80g (2½oz)	25	1
Buckwheat, cooked 80g (2½oz)	54	0
Bulgur, cooked 120g (4oz)	48	1
Cornmeal (polenta) 120g (4oz)	68	1
Couscous, cooked 120g (4oz)	65	0
Maize (polenta), 40g (1½oz)	68	1
Millet, cooked 120g (4oz)	71	0
Polenta cooked 120g (4oz)	68	0
Tapioca, steamed 100g (3½oz)	70	6

Rice

Rice	GI	Fat
Arborio risotto white boiled 100g (3½oz)	69	0
Basmati white boiled 180g (2½oz)	58	0
Broken white steamed 180g (2½oz)	86	0
Calrose, white cooked 180g (2½oz)	87	1
Doongara, white cooked 180g (2½oz)	59	0
Glutinous, white steamed 174g (2½oz)	98	0
Instant cooked 180g (2½oz)	87	0
Jasmine white steamed 180g (2½oz)	109	0
Pelde, brown boiled 180g (2½oz)	76	0
Sun brown quick boiled 180g (2½oz)	80	0

Cookies and biscuits

Cookies and biscuits	GI	Fat
Digestives plain 2 cookies	59	6
Graham wafers, 4 biscuits	74	3
Milk Arrowroot, 2 biscuits	69	2
Morning coffee, 3 biscuits	79	2
Oatmeal, 2 biscuits	55	3
Rich tea, 2 biscuits	55	3
Shortbread, 2 biscuits	64	8
Shredded wheat, 2 biscuits	62	2
Vanilla wafers, 6 biscuits	77	5

Crackers

Crackers	GI	Fat
Brenton Wheat Crackers 6 biscuits	67	6
Corn cakes, 2	87	0
Jatz, 6 biscuits	55	5
Kavli, 4 biscuits	71	0
Premium soda crackers, 3 biscuts	74	4

	GI	Fat
Puffed crisp bread, 4 biscuits	81	1
Rice cakes, 2	82	1
Ryvita, 2 slices	69	1
Sao, 3 biscuits	70	4
Stoned wheat thins, 5 biscuits	67	2
Water crackers, 5 biscuits	78	2

Dairy foods

	GI	Fat
Chocolate pudding 100g (3½oz)	49	4
Condensed milk 160g (5½oz)	61	15
Custard 175g (6oz)	43	5
Custard, powder 100g (3½oz)	35	5
Ice cream, Sara Lee Vanilla 100ml (3fl oz)	38	16
Ice cream, full fat, 50g (1½oz)	61	6
Ice cream, low fat, 50g (1½oz)	50	2
Ice cream, Sara Lee chocolate, 100ml (3fl oz)	37	15
Milk, full fat 250ml (8fl oz)	27	10
Milk, skim 250ml (8fl oz)	32	0
Vaalia yoghurt drink 150ml (5fl oz)	69	1
Vaalia, Apricot & Mango 200g (7oz)	26	2
Vaalia, French Vanilla 200g (7oz)	26	3
Vaalia, no-fat, Vanilla 200g (7oz)	23	0
Vaalia, no-fat, Mango 200g (7oz)	23	0
Vaalia, no-fat, Mixed berry 200g (7oz)	25	0
Vaalia, no-fat, Strawberry 200g (7oz)	23	0
Yakult, 65ml serve (¼cup)	46	0
Yoghurt, extra lite, Strawberry 200g (7oz)	28	2
Yoghurt, low fat, fruit 200g (7oz)	33	0
Yoghurt, sweetener 200g (7oz)	14	0

Fruit	GI	Fat
Apple, medium 150g (1½oz)	38	0
Apricots fresh, 100g (3½oz)	57	0
Apricots, canned, 125g (4oz)	72	0
Apricots, dried 3-6 pieces 30g (1oz)	31	0
Banana raw 150g (1½oz)	55	0
Breadfruit 120g (4oz)	68	1
Cherries 20 cherries, 80g (2½oz)	22	0
Custard apple, fresh 120g (4oz)	54	1
Dates, dried 40g (1½oz)	103	0
Figs dried, 50g (1½oz)	61	<1
Grapefruit raw 100g (3½oz)	25	0
Grapes, green 100g (3½oz)	46	0
Kiwifruit, raw 80g (2½oz)	52	0
Lychee, canned 90g (3oz)	79	0
Mango, small 150g (1½oz)	55	0
Orange, medium 130g (1oz)	44	0
Papaw, 200g (7oz)	83	0
Peach, canned 125g (4oz)	59	0
Peach, fresh 100g (3½oz)	42	0
Pear, canned 125g (4oz)	43	0
Pear, fresh 150g (5oz)	38	0
Pineapple 125g (4oz)	52	0
Plum 100g (3½oz)	55	0
Prunes, fresh, 40g (1½oz)	29	0
Raisins, 40g (1½oz)	64	0
Rockmelon 200g (7oz)	65	0
Strawberries 100g (3½oz)	35	0
Sultanas 40g (1½oz)	56	0
Watermelon 150g (1½oz)	72	0

Legumes

Legumes	GI	Fat
Baked beans, boiled 120g(4oz)	30	1
Black-eyed beans, boiled 120g (4oz)	42	1
Broad beans, fava 80g (2½oz)	79	1
Butter beans, boiled 70g (2¼oz)	31	0
Chickpeas, boiled 120g (4oz)	33	3
Chickpeas, canned 95g (3oz)	42	2
Haricot/navy beans 95g (3oz)	38	1
Kidney beans, boiled 90g (3oz)	27	0
Kidney beans, canned 95g (3oz)	52	0
Lentils, brown & brown 95g (3oz)	30	0
Lentils, red, boiled, 120g (4oz)	26	1
Lima beans, baby frozen 85g (2¾oz)	32	0
Pinto beans, boiled 95g (3oz)	39	0
Pinto beans, canned 90g (3oz)	45	0
Romano beans, boiled 90g (3oz)	46	0
Soya beans, boiled 90g (3oz)	18	7
Soya beans, canned 100g (3½oz)	14	6
Split peas yellow canned 220ml (7½oz)	60	2
Split peas, yellow boiled 90g (3oz)	32	0

Pasta

Pasta	GI	Fat
Capellini, cooked 180g (2½oz)	45	0
Corn pasta, dry 63g (2oz)	78	1
Fettuccine, cooked 180g (2½oz)	32	1
Gnocchi, cooked 145g (4¾oz)	68	3
Linguine thick, cooked 180g (2½oz)	46	1
Linguine thin, cooked 180g (2½oz)	55	1
Macaroni and cheese, cooked 85g (2¾oz)	64	24

	GI	Fat
Macaroni, cooked 180g (2½oz)	45	1
Noodles, 2 minute 85g (2½oz)	46	16
Noodles, mung bean 140g (1½oz)	39	0
Noodles, rice, boiled 176g (5¾oz)	40	0
Ravioli, meat filled, cooked 220g (7oz)	39	11
Rice pasta, brown, cooked 180g (2½oz)	92	2
Rice vermicelli, cooked 180g (2½oz)	58	0
Ris o mais gluten free dry 63g (2oz)	76	0
Soy pasta, dry, 63g (2oz)	29	1
Spaghetti wholemeal cooked 180g (2½oz)	38	1
Spaghetti, white, cooked 180g (2½oz)	41	1
Spirali, durum, cooked 180g (2½oz)	43	1
Star pastina, cooked 180g (2½oz)	38	1
Tortellini, cheese, cooked 180g (2½oz)	50	8
Vermicelli, cooked 180g (2½oz)	35	0

Vegetables

	GI	Fat
Beetroot, canned 60g (2oz)	64	0
Carrots, boiled 70g (2¼oz)	49	0
Desiree, boiled 90g (3oz)	101	0
French Fries, fine cut, 120g (4oz)	75	26
Parsnips, boiled 75g (2½oz)	97	0
Peas, dried boiled 70g (2¼oz)	22	0
Peas, green fresh 80g (2¼oz)	48	0
Pontiac, boiled 120g (4oz)	88	0
Potato microwave 120g (4oz)	79	0
Potato, baked 120g (4oz)	93	0
Potato, canned 175g (5¾oz)	65	0
Potato, instant ½ cup	83	1
Potato, mashed no fat 120g (4oz)	91	0

	GI	Fat
Potato, new, boiled 175g (5¾oz)	78	0
Potato, steamed 120g (4oz)	80	0
Pumpkin boiled 85g (2¾oz)	75	0
Swede, boiled 120g (4oz)	72	0
Sweet corn, canned 40g (1½oz)	55	1
Sweet potato (yam), boiled 80g (2½oz)	54	0
Taro, boiled, 80g (2½oz)	54	0
Yam, boiled 80g (2½oz)	51	0

Snack foods

	GI	Fat
Chocolate, Milky Bar white 55g (2oz)	44	18
Chocolate, Nestle Milk, 60g (2oz)	42	9
Corn chips, Doritos 50g (1½oz)	42	11
Burger Rings 50g (1½oz)	90	13
Chicken nuggets 100g (3½oz)	46	16
Fruit cocktail canned 125g (4oz)	55	0
Jams, strawberry, 1 tablespoon	51	0
Jelly beans, 5	80	0
M&M (peanut), 50g (1½oz) pkt	33	13
Marmalade, 1 tablespoon	48	0
Mars Bar, 60g (2oz)	65	11
Mousse, reduced fat 100g (3½oz)	32	2
Muesli bars w/fruit, 30g (1oz)	61	4
Nutella spread, 1 tablespoon	33	6
Peanuts, roasted, salted, 75g (2½oz)	14	40
Popcorn, low fat, 1 tablespoon	55	2
Potato crisps, plain, 50g (1½oz)	54	16
Power Bar, Performance 65g (2oz)	58	5
Pretzels, 50g (1½oz)	83	1
Snicker, 59g (2oz)	41	14

	GI	Fat
Taco shells, 2 shells	68	6
Tofu frozen desert, 100g (3½oz)	115	1

Soups

	GI	Fat
Black bean soup, 220ml (7oz)	64	2
Green pea soup, can 220ml (7oz)	66	1
Lentil soup, can 220ml (7oz)	44	0
Split pea soup, can 220ml (7oz)	60	2
Tomato soup, can 220ml (7oz)	38	1

Sugars

	GI	Fat
Agave nectar, 1 tablespoon	11	0
Fructose, 1 teaspoon	23	0
Glucose tablets, 1 tablespoon	112	0
Glucose, 1 teaspoon	102	0
Honey, 1 teaspoon	58	0
Lactose, 1 teaspoon	6	0
Maltose, 1 teaspoon	105	0
Sucrose, 1 teaspoon	65	0

☞ Tip

You need to drink 2–3 litres of water a day but that can get a little boring. Instead of diet or normal soft drinks, keep a bottle of water with fresh mint, orange, lemon, lime and grated ginger.

Glossary of Nutritional Foods

Commonly available in healthfood stores and supermarkets

Agar is often used as a thickening agent.

Agave nectar is made from the Agave cactus. It tastes and pours like honey but is 1.5 times sweeter than sugar. It is a fructose sweetener and a complex carbohydrate.

Alaria is an edible seaweed

Amaranth is a grain containing 50 per cent more protein than most other grains and contains no gluten. It is produced as a flour, puffed grain or as porridge.

Black beans are a type of legume. They are small, oval beans with a shiny, black skin and a tender texture. They have an earthy mushroom flavour.

Buckwheat is not a grain, but a fruit kernel. It is mainly used for making pancakes.

Liquid Amino is a delicious and nutritious alternative to soy sauce and tamari. Made only from non-GMO soy beans and purified water, it contains no preservatives, colouring agents or chemicals. It is not fermented or heated and is gluten free. It is also much lower in sodium than other soy sauce.

Carob powder is used as a substitute for cocoa or chocolate.

Chinese mushrooms are edible mushrooms with a fantastic earthy flavour.

Chlorella is a form of green algae found in still, fresh water, soil or the bark of trees. It is high in iron and protein.

Couscous is a cereal product made from semolina, steamed and coated with flour.

Dulse is a type of red algae high in iodine. You can buy it at most health food stores.

Flaxseed (linseed) comes in the form of a seed or meal. It is high in protein and essential fatty acids.

Full-grain bread has a variety of unprocessed grains mixed with a wheat or wholemeal flour. It is high in fibre and lower GI than most white or wholemeal breads.

The glycemic index is a means of rating the effect that a particular food has on blood sugar levels. Foods that cause a rapid rise in blood sugar (and consequently an excessive release of insulin) are known as 'high glycemic foods'. Conversely, 'low glycemic foods' cause a slower, sustained increase in blood sugar and insulin.

Harissa is a fiery chilli sauce used extensively in North African cooking.

Kelp is a type of algae. Known as a sea vegetable, it's used as seaweed. It is high in iodine and protein and is available from health food stores and Japanese markets.

Kombu is a dark green sea vegetable from the kelp family. Used in Japanese cooking, it is an essential ingredient of dashi, a flavourful stock. Kombu contains significant amounts of glutamic acid, the basis of monosodium glutamate (MSG).

Lecithin is a commercially produced combination of phospholipids and fatty acids extracted (usually) from soybeans or sometimes egg yolk. It can be purchased as powder, granules or capsules.

LSA is a mix of linseeds, sunflower seed and almonds. It is high in essential fatty acids and protein and is wonderful sprinkled over cereals, salads or in smoothies.

Millet is a type of cereal grain that can be used in breakfast cereals or salads.

Mirin is a type of Japanese rice wine. Originally used as drinking alcohol, it is an essential part of Japanese cooking.

Miso is a fermented soybean product with added rice or barley. It can be used as a soup, stock or sauce base. It has a salty flavour.

Miso tempeh is an easily digested, processed, chunky-textured cake of cooked fermented soybeans used like tofu.

Multigrain bread is the same as full-grain bread.

Natural plain yoghurt is yoghurt that is less processed and has no sugar added.

Nori is a type of red algae that is commonly used as a sea vegetable. It is usually sold commercially in the form of flat sheets of the type used in the preparation of sushi.

Oats are a type of cereal grain containing gluten. Oats are excellent as porridge or in cooking and are produced as either oatmeal, oat bran, rolled oats or oat flour.

Pepitas are edible pumpkin seeds. They are high in zinc and protein.

Psyllium is a husk used as a form of insoluble fibre. It is excellent for digestion.

Quinoa is a South American grain high in protein and Vitamins Bs. It contains no gluten. It is produced in the form of flour, flakes or puffed grains.

Rice flour is rice ground into flour. It contains no gluten.

Rice wine vinegar is vinegar made from rice. It has a sweet and sour taste.

Rye is a type of cereal grain. It contains gluten.

Sake is Japanese drinking rice wine.

Spelt flour is made from the spelt wheat grain.

Spirulina is a blue-green algae very high in protein and iron. Can be used as a health supplement or added to food it should be heated.

Soy milk is made from soaking and grinding soybeans and adding water. It contains no lactose but some may contain gluten.

Soy protein powder is made from soybean protein and is an excellent alternative to whey protein. It contains no dairy.

Sweet potato (yam) is a root vegetable. It has a lower GI than potatoes and can be cooked in the same way.

Tahini is a paste made from sesame seeds.

Tamari is a wheat-free soy sauce.

Tandoori powder is an Indian cooking powder used in the tandoor cooking process.

Tempeh (same as soy tempeh).

Tofu is also known as a soybean curd. It is the processed form of soya beans and is made into hard or silkened tofu.

Trans fatty acids or hydrogenate fats are the heated form of fats or oils. They are hard for the body to break down and are believed to be carcinogenic.

Verjuice is made from grapes and is really wine without the alcohol. Its fresh taste makes it excellent in sauces.

Wakame is a flat sea vegetable used in Japanese cooking.

Wheatgerm is a cereal grain. It is a fantastic source of fibre, vitamin E and essential fatty acids. It can be added to smoothies, muffins, pancakes and cereals.

Whey protein powder is the protein and amino acid extracted from whey. It does contain lactose in most cases. It is a fantastic dietary protein.

Wild rice is a type of cereal grain that's chewier and smokier than conventional rice.

Wholegrains are unprocessed grains that are slower to digest.

Wholegrain bread is the same as full-grain bread.

Index